What Every Mormon Needs to See

by Jeff Kliewer

ISBN-10: 0692338276
ISBN-13: 978-0692338278

DEDICATION

To the young Mormon men on mission to Philadelphia, all of whom have a Bible in their possession and some of whom are open to having their vision tested by the Word of God to know whether or not they see the truth, that they not be found to be blind guides.

CONTENTS

ACKNOWLEDGEMENTS

I am very grateful to MormonThink.com, Adam's Road Band, Micah Wilder, New Name Noah, Youtube channels ptyler3 and MormonHistoryBuff, Living Hope Ministries, CARM, mrm.org, Alpha and Omega Ministries, Utah Lighthouse Ministry, exmormon.org and many others whose research posted online contributed greatly to the content of this book. The excellent and well-documented research of those listed above provided many of the facts that I felt called to write about.

INTRODUCTION

Mormons have been taught to trust themselves rather than the Bible to decide what is true. They think that their testimony is the infallible testimony of God and anything that opposes it is only the fallible testimony of man[1]. The inward conviction in the heart of the individual, especially the individual reader of the Book of Mormon, is the only standard of truth that Mormons believe to be infallible. They are taught that outside evidences can bolster faith, but once God Himself has spoken to an individual heart, no evidence on earth could overthrow what the individual Mormon has heard Him say. This indoctrination begins in the Introduction to the Book of Mormon.

We invite all men everywhere to read the Book of Mormon, to ponder in their hearts the message it contains, and then to ask God, the Eternal Father, in the name of Christ if the book is true. Those who pursue this course and ask in faith will gain a testimony of its truth and divinity by the power of the Holy Ghost. (See Moroni 10:3-5.) Those who gain this divine witness from the Holy Spirit will also come to know by the same power that Jesus Christ is the Savior of the world, that Joseph Smith is His revelator and prophet in these last days, and that The Church of Jesus Christ of Latter-day Saints is the Lord's kingdom once again established on the earth, preparatory to the Second Coming of the Messiah[2].

---

[1] See Appendix A. Mormon teachings about how God brings people to know the truth is the fundamental deception that prevents Mormons from openly and honestly pursuing the truth.

[2] I read the Book of Mormon. I pondered the message it contains. Then I asked God, the Eternal Father, in the name of Christ, for supernatural wisdom to help me understand the truth about the Book of Mormon and speak the truth without fear or compromise. I believe that God gave me wisdom (James 1:5) to write a Review of the Book of Mormon. Please see Appendix B.

If someone follows this prescribed course of action and then something happens within the person's heart that he or she believes to be a fulfillment of the promise of Moroni 10:3-5, then that individual is locked in. The person's experience is no ordinary event (or series of events) in his or her life. He or she has a category for the experience—the one given by the Book of Mormon. If that person thinks that "this divine witness from the Holy Spirit" has happened to him or her, it takes on a life of its own. Nothing more need be said. Joseph Smith need not be tested (meaning that 1 John 4:1 need not be obeyed). God has spoken. What could man add to that?

The great deception involved here is that God has not spoken any such authoritative revelations to the hearts of individual Mormons. I would echo what the Holy Spirit said through Paul to Titus, who had a special calling that required strong discernment.

For this reason I left you in Crete, that you would set in order what remains and appoint elders in every city as I directed you, namely if any man is above reproach, the husband of one wife, having children who believe, not accused of dissipation or rebellion. For the overseer must be above reproach as God's steward, not self-willed, not quick-tempered, not addicted to wine, not pugnacious, not fond of sordid gain, but hospitable, loving what is good, sensible, just, devout, self-controlled, holding fast the faithful word which is in accordance with the teaching, so that he will be able both to exhort in sound doctrine and to refute those who contradict (Titus 1:5-9).

Since God spoke the words of the Bible, the inner impressions that God places on the hearts of individuals will never contradict what we find in the Bible. For example, God will never give an inner impression *"that Joseph Smith is His revelator and prophet in these last days"* if Joseph Smith had about 32 wives, since God already said that just to be an elder, one must be the husband of but *one wife*. Should the last-days revelator and prophet have a different standard than other elders/overseers? Because God spoke Titus 1 to the New Testament Church[3], the fact that Smith had many wives is—by itself—proof that

---

Please read it, think about it, pray about it, and search the Bible to see if these things are so.
[3] At times, before Jesus came, God was willing to overlook polygamy. But when Jesus spoke, God reaffirmed exclusively monogamous marriage, in accordance with the created order. Concerning divorce, Jesus referenced the created order, saying "For this reason a man shall leave his father and mother and be joined to his wife, and the two shall become one flesh" (Matthew 19:5). For a time, Moses permitted a man "to divorce his wife" (19:8), but this less-than-ideal allowance had something to do with "your hardness of heart" (19:8). Similarly, for whatever reason God allowed polygamy in the Old Testament, it was a less-than-ideal allowance. Paul's point to Titus still stands to this day. If a man is married to more than "one

inner impressions confirming Smith are not from God. Likewise, since Smith was *fond of sordid gain* and never resolved the damage he caused in his banking scandal in Ohio[4], he had a bad reputation. Since Smith was often *accused of dissipation or rebellion*, he didn't meet the Biblical requirement that *the overseer must be above reproach as God's steward*[5].

The bottom line of what we learn from the Book of Titus is that Truth is known by those who are *holding fast the faithful word*, not by those whose private experience contradicts what was written therein. The Bible contains *sound doctrine* and by remaining *in accordance with the teaching* of the Bible, those who hold fast to the Bible can *refute those who contradict*. In other words, Biblical revelations, rather than private experiences, are the arbiters of truth.

Epistemology is the study of how we know things. The Book of Mormon teaches an epistemological foundation that is based upon the human heart. But how much can we trust our own inner impressions? Long before the Book of Mormon told us to trust our hearts, God told us not to trust our hearts. To trust our hearts is to trust ourselves rather than God.

The heart is more deceitful than all else and is desperately sick; who can understand it? (Jeremiah 17:9)

The Bible teaches an epistemological foundation based upon the Word of God. Something is true if it is *in accordance with* (Titus 1:9) what God says in the Old Testament and New Testament. That is why the first book of the New Testament quotes the Old Testament more than 60 times. The New Testament authors are always concerned about demonstrating the analogue that exists between their new revelation and the revelation that preceded them. That is also why the Biblical tests of a prophet are so important. God did not give them in order for them to be ignored. He did not elevate private impressions placed upon the

---

wife" (Titus 1:6), then he is not qualified to be an elder. If not an elder, then he isn't a "seer".

[4] http://mormonthink.com/glossary/anti-banking.htm

[5] Joseph Smith was involved in at least 10 cases of polyandry—he married women who were still married to another husband. Not only so, primary sources allege Smith's sexual misconduct in cases relating to Eliza Winters, Marinda Nancy Johnson, Vienna Jacques, "a Miss Hill", Fanny Alger, Lucinda Harris, Sarah Pratt, Melissa Schindle, Catherine Fuller Warren, Helen Mar Kimball, Sylvia Sessions, Eliza Snow, Melissa Lott, Almera Johnson, Eliza Partridge, Emily Partridge, Louisa Beaman, Lucy Walker, Maria and Sarah Lawrence, Sarah Ann Whitney, and Olive Frost (Mormonthink.com/grant6.htm). Titus 1:6 would advise investigating these charges rather than letting feelings grant Smith authority as the elder-prophet-seer who restores the Church.

deceitful and desperately sick human heart above His Word. He said He holds His Word above His own Name (Psalm 138:2). That means that the unchangeableness of the Bible is backed up by the unchangeableness of God's own nature.

Sanctify them in the truth; Your word is truth (John 17:17)

Truth is determined and comes to be known by the Bible. Since Joseph Smith fails the Biblical tests of a prophet, personal experiences in the human heart that confirm that Joseph Smith is a prophet are not the testimony of God. Alternative explanations better suit the facts of the individual Mormon experience.

First, most Mormons want the Book of Mormon to be true when they set out in pursuit of their testimony. I have spoken to many Mormons and often ask them to share their testimony with me. Whether they were raised by Mormons or have something else already invested, it is usually already in the self-interest of the sign-seeker that Mormonism prove to be true. If you want something, it doesn't take much for the sinful human heart to convince itself that God has granted that desire.

Second, the "burning in the bosom" is not unique to Mormons. It is the same standard for measuring truth that Muslims use. The effect that the Qur'an has upon their hearts mirrors what the Book of Mormon does to the Mormon. Listen to Muslim Mullahs cry as they recite their book. They test its truth by the emotion it provokes in them. Profound emotion accompanies virtually every religious truth claim in the world. The human heart is capable of producing the deepest and fiercest passions.

Third, remember that the Book of Mormon contains a great deal of truth, because it borrows a great deal from the Bible! As I read through it, this is what struck me most. If Joseph Smith places Jesus in the New World and places many of Jesus' own Biblical words in His mouth, then are those words emptied of their power? Something of the truth of God will transcend the error of the self-attesting prophet. In so far as the Book of Mormon marches alongside of the teachings of the Bible, it echoes the truth of the Bible. But this is a two-edged sword, because the reader who hears truth in the Book of Mormon learns to trust the Book and derails with it when it departs from the Biblical teaching. What is most scary is how nearly orthodox—even Trinitarian—the Book of Mormon is. It was later (D&C 132, the Book of Abraham of the Pearl of Great Price, the Elder King Follett Discourse in the Journal of

Discourses) that Smith introduced his most damnable heresies.

For such men are false apostles, deceitful workers, disguising themselves as apostles of Christ. No wonder, for even Satan disguises himself as an angel of light. Therefore it is not surprising if his servants also disguise themselves as servants of righteousness, whose end will be according to their deeds (2 Corinthians 11:13-15)

What Every Mormon Needs to See began as a letter to Mormon missionaries stationed a few blocks from where I serve as a Christian missionary to Philadelphia. God led me and one of my brothers in Christ to go to their outreach center for the purpose of witnessing to them. Like the Apostle Paul, we were sent "to open their eyes so that they may turn from darkness to light and from the dominion of Satan to God, that they may receive the forgiveness of sins and an inheritance among those who have been sanctified by faith in [Christ]" (Acts 26:18).

Trouble is, they didn't immediately believe that it was really God who sent us. So, I decided to write them a letter to follow up on our conversation, citing the Bible. It turned into a book. Hopefully what follows will be helpful to anyone who looks to Joseph Smith as God's prophet. Furthermore, anyone who loves the truth will be glad to know the seven Biblical tests of a prophet employed in this book. In these latter days, many false prophets will arise (Matthew 24:24), so it will be increasingly important to know *how* to test the spirits (1 John 4:1).

Dear Elder,

The Bible provides certain tests by which we can know if Joseph Smith was a genuine prophet sent by God. I understand that as a Mormon, you already have a testimony that affirms that Joseph was a prophet. But may I ask you a question: Do you believe **all** the genuine prophets who went before Joseph? I know that you do. But do you know that **Moses** and **Jesus** provided several distinct tests by which all later prophets were to be judged? Joseph Smith did not deny that Moses and Jesus were prophets, so will you entertain the application of these seven tests that God revealed through them, if even for the purpose of reinforcing your own testimony?

When I came to you last week, I didn't expect you to just blindly accept the message I brought. Because I came preaching the Person of Jesus Christ and the sufficiency of His death and resurrection for the salvation of all who believe, I hoped you would receive it for the good news that it is. But I also expected you to test what I said.

In the same way, it is commendable to test Joseph Smith. If he is a genuine prophet, then surely he will shine forth under the light of the Biblical tests that God provided. If by these tests, he proves himself false, then all is not lost for you. Jesus remains the Light of the world and the Source of eternal life into which you can run. Whichever way it turns out, prophets need to be tested. Faith is not blind.

The Bereans were commended for listening to the new message of the Apostle Paul while at the same time giving the highest respect to the old message of the Law, the Writings, and the Prophets. "Now these were more noble-minded than those in Thessalonica, for they received the word with great eagerness, examining the Scriptures daily to see whether these things were so" (Acts 17:11). We can learn from the Bereans that there is nothing to fear when turning to the Scriptures. Surely one does not put the Lord to the test by employing the very tests the Lord gave us in His Book. He would call it noble if you spent many days examining Scriptures to see—first of all—if these tests of a prophet are really there in the Bible, and—secondly—if Joseph Smith passes them.

You thought it necessary to *test the Spirit* with which I came to you. That's good. We are commanded to test anyone who presumes to speak for God. "Beloved, do not believe every spirit, but test the spirits to see whether they are from God, because many false prophets have gone out into the world" (1 John 4:1). Are you willing to test the spirit of Joseph Smith, provided the tests themselves come from the Bible?

Moses and Jesus are two trustworthy prophets, Jesus being a prophet and so much more. Will you trust them enough to apply seven of their tests for truth in order to weigh Joseph Smith in the Biblical balance?

The first biblical test is for **consistency**. It comes through Moses in Deuteronomy 13:1-3. "If a prophet or a dreamer of dreams arises among you and gives you a sign or a wonder, and the sign or the wonder comes true, concerning which he spoke to you, saying, 'Let us go after other gods (whom you have not known) and let us serve them,' you shall not listen to the words of that prophet or that dreamer of dreams; for the Lord your God is testing you to find out if you love the Lord your God with all your heart and with all your soul." Since Joseph Smith claimed special revelations and a miraculous recovery of golden plates with these revelations inscribed thereupon, we must test these revelations to see if they are consistent with earlier ones. Is the new revelator preaching a different God (or gods)?

The second biblical test is for **predictions**. Moses spoke prophetically in Deuteronomy 18:20-22. "But the prophet who speaks a word presumptuously in My name which I have not commanded him to speak, or which he speaks in the name of other gods, that prophet shall die. You may say in your heart, 'How will we know the word which the Lord has not spoken?' When a prophet speaks in the name of the Lord, if the thing does not come about or come true, that is the thing which the Lord has not spoken. The prophet has spoken it presumptuously; you shall not be afraid of him." This test is quite amazing because it can only be applied *if* a self-proclaimed prophet makes predictions in the name of the Lord, which—interestingly—self-attesting prophets always seem to do. Muhammad made several predictions. Some required one hundred years to pass before they could be tested definitively. Joseph Smith's predictions required a generation, but like Muhammad's, they are testable now.

The third biblical test is for **fruit**. Jesus was concerned to protect us, so He pointed to something obvious that would expose something hidden. "Beware of the false prophets, who come to you in sheep's clothing, but inwardly are ravenous wolves. You will know them by their fruits. Grapes are not gathered from thorn bushes nor figs from thistles, are they? So every good tree bears good fruit, but the bad tree bears bad fruit" (Matthew 7:15-17). False prophets may have amazing abilities that hide their true identity. They may prophesy, cast out demons, and perform miracles (Matthew 7:22), but this is not proof that they belong to Christ. The obvious sign that reveals the hidden identity of false prophets is when their sins find them out. Test them for moral failures without repentance.

The fourth biblical test is for **miracles**. As Jesus warned in Matthew 7:22, the presence of what appear to be supernatural occurrences are no proof positive that a prophet genuinely comes from God. But the expectation with which Moses left us and the fulfillment that Jesus claimed for Himself would indicate that the absence of clear signs and wonders makes a liar of anyone that would claim to supersede both Moses and Jesus. The Torah ends with an eye out for a miracle-working prophet—one even greater than Moses (Deuteronomy 34:10-12). Later, Jesus validated Himself by His undeniably great miracles. "Believe because of the works themselves" (John 14:11). If the Book of Mormon, Doctrine and Covenants, and Pearl of Great Price are trustworthy sources while the Law of Moses and words of Jesus allegedly have proven to be corruptible, then did Joseph Smith have clear miracles to mark him as a greater prophet than both Moses and Jesus?

The fifth biblical test is for **measures**. False prophets rarely appeal to the Biblical tests of a prophet. Rather, they establish themselves by their own basis of authority. But even this the Bible anticipates, and meeting the false prophets on their own ground, it exposes them by their own standard. Joseph Smith judges the entire Christian Church guilty of falling into apostasy and appeals to private inward confirmations as proof for his body of teaching (Moroni 10:3-5). Jesus said, "Do not judge so that you will not be judged. For in the way you judge, you will be judged; and by your standard of measure, it will be measured to you" (Matthew 7:1-2). What would the outcome be if private confirmations were a test for truth, even though they are not?

The sixth test for the truthfulness of a prophet is **accuracy**. Often, religious claims are not falsifiable. They speak of things from another world, beyond the faculties of our five senses. Whereas these cannot be disproven, the things of this world can be tested. Jesus taught about the new birth, a spiritual reality that results in very noticeable changes in the life of the person who has it. If Nicodemus couldn't track with Jesus through His teaching concerning the starting point of eternal life, then there would be no sense in moving on to teaching anything more about things to come. "If I told you earthly things and you do not believe, how will you believe if I tell you heavenly things" (John 3:12)? Conversely, if a prophet fails to speak accurately when telling about earthly things, how can he be trusted when he speaks about heavenly things? Did Joseph Smith speak falsely when he spoke about things that are falsifiable, things of this world, things that can be tested?

Seventh and finally, the Bible tests **motives**. Jesus was genuinely the King of Kings and Lord of Lords, yet His actions and teachings revealed the most selfless motive. "For even the Son of Man did not come to be served, but to serve, and to give His life a ransom for many" (Mark 10:45). His bloody death on Calvary's tree was the purest demonstration of the evident motives of his heart. Truly, people cannot hide their motives forever. What Jesus said as a Prophet benefitted the entire world of humanity—not his own flesh. Did the prophecies allegedly given to Joseph Smith betray any self-serving fleshly motives?

Joseph Smith made some fantastic claims. He didn't simply offer another testimony about Jesus Christ, the way Christians for two thousand years have witnessed to the glory of the Son of God and His amazing grace. Rather, he proposed that the church was in apostasy from the death of the last Apostle until the arrival of Joseph Smith. He claimed to have a restored gospel. He brought many teachings that he said he recovered—God the Father, or Elohim, was once a man. He resides near the planet Kolob. Jesus, also known as Jehovah, is an offspring from Elohim's eternal marriage. Lucifer was Jesus' brother. The way of salvation includes doing what one can do, grace kicking in after that. Men can progress to become gods of other worlds through eternal marriage, worthy living, Temple rites, etc.—If ever there was a need to apply the Biblical tests of a prophet, then surely the teachings of Joseph Smith beg for them now.

CHAPTER 1

THE FIRST BIBLICAL TEST OF A PROPHET:
CONSISTENCY

DEUTERONOMY 13:1-3

According to Joseph Smith, the book of Mormon is a consistent continuation of the earlier revelations found in the Bible. "For behold, this is written for the intent that ye may believe that; and if ye believe that ye will believe this also" (Mormon 7:9). The author of such an assertion, be it Mormon or Smith, understands the plainest of all tests for truth—that of consistency. The God who authored an earlier book could at no place contradict Himself in a later revelation. He is free to change the economy under which He deals with men. He is free to tell us things we never knew before. But as to those things which He Himself described as unchangeable in an earlier revelation, no changes are possible. The Deuteronomy 13:1-3 test is supremely concerned with the nature of God, which it will be shown is the most unchangeable of all things. Yet, at this point exactly, Smith's later revelations contradict what God revealed earlier.

The earlier revelation conveys the singularity and transcendence of the one true God (Deuteronomy 6:4). There is only one God! He is eternally existent—the Alpha and Omega (Revelation 1:8, 22:13). He has no beginning, but rather, has always been precisely who He is. "I am who I am" (Exodus 3:14). "In the beginning" (Genesis 1:1), there was only "God". He doesn't change like mortal men do (Malachi 3:6). He is all-powerful (Genesis 18:14). He is Three-in-one (1 Corinthians 12:4-6), and as such, He is complete and entirely satisfied within Himself. He has need of nothing (Acts 17:25). He has a will and perfectly brings it to pass (Psalm 138:8). He is all-knowing (Hebrews 4:13). He is greater than His creation by a factor of infinity (Psalm 113:4-6). Nothing exists apart from that which He has made (John 1:3). All creation exists for His glory (Revelation 4:11). The Deuteronomy 13:1-3 test requires all future prophets to remain consistent with these earlier revelations of who God is.

Joseph Smith's later revelations, being now subject to the test, propose an infinite regression and eternal progression of gods. Smith denies Deuteronomy 6:4 in his reformulation of the Trinity, saying "these three constitute three distinct personages and three Gods" (Teachings of Prophet Joseph Smith, p. 370). Speaking of the Father, Smith claims that He was once a man, and concerning certain men, Smith proposes that they can progress to become gods.

Hence, the doctrine of a plurality of Gods is as prominent in the Bible as any other doctrine (History of the Church, vol. 6, p. 474)

In the beginning, the head of the Gods called a council of the Gods; and they came together and concocted a plan to create the world and people it (Journal of Discourses, vol. 6, p. 5)

God himself was once as we are now, and is an exalted Man, and sits enthroned in yonder heavens...I say, if you were to see him today, you would see him like a man in form—like yourselves, in all the person, image, and very form as a man...it is necessary that we should understand the very character and being of God, and how He came to be so; for I am going to tell you how God came to be God. We have imagined and supposed that God was God from all eternity, I will refute that idea, and will take away and do away the veil, so that you may see...and that he was once a man like us; yea, that God himself the Father of us all, dwelt on an earth the same as Jesus Christ himself did (Journal of Discourses, vol. 6, p. 3)

These teachings of Joseph Smith are plainly polytheistic. He speaks explicitly about a multiplicity of gods—not just God (singular) but gods (plural). He has God the Father evolving over time. He makes God less than omniscient and omnipotent. He essentially brings God down to our level. But remember the earlier prophets, who prophesied thus.

Bring out the people who are blind, even though they have eyes, and the deaf, even though they have ears. All the nations have gathered together so that the peoples may be assembled. Who among them can declare this and proclaim to us the former things? Let them present their witnesses that they may be justified, or let them hear and say, "It is true." "You are My witnesses," declares the Lord, "and My servant whom I have chosen, so that you may know and believe Me and understand that I am He. Before Me there was no God formed, and there will be none after Me. I, even I, am the Lord, and there is no savior besides Me (Isaiah 43:8-11).

Let the self-proclaimed prophet speak of former things. If he can agree with Isaiah and say "It is true", then allow him a seat at the table to continue a conversation. But if he stands to "refute that idea" and if he then *denies* that "God was God from all eternity", then recognize immediately that this self-proclaimed prophet is spiritually blind and deaf. He has spoken presumptuously concerning the very nature of God. Every prophet in the Old and New Testament, including Moses in Deuteronomy 4:35 and Jesus in Mark 12:29, agreed that there is only One God, He was never formed, and there will be none after Him (Isaiah 43:10).

Joseph Smith therefore fails the consistency test by speaking in opposition to what Jesus said was the foremost of all the commandments. "Jesus answered, "The foremost is, 'Hear, O Israel! The Lord our God is One Lord" (Mark 12:29). That Joseph Smith fails at this particular point is no trivial matter, nor is it a coincidence that this would be a point of Smith's departure. The God who gave us the Deuteronomy 13:1-3 test allowed Joseph Smith to speak of "other gods" (plural) in order to test your devotion to Yahweh (Deuteronomy 13:3).

We move on to Joseph Smith's new revelations concerning the second member of the Trinity. Are they consistent with what God revealed through earlier prophets?

In the beginning was the Word, and the Word was with God, and the Word was God (John 1:1)

Jesus said to him, "Have I been so long with you, and yet you have not come to know Me, Philip? He who has seen Me has seen the Father" (John 14:9)

The earlier revelation clearly reveals that Jesus is God. He is not a procreation of the Father but has always been equal with the Father, because He is One Essence with the Father. The Father, the Son, and the Holy Spirit are only one God—the Creator of everything else that exists. But what do Smith's later revelations say about Jesus?

And now, verily I [Christ] say unto you, I was in the beginning with the Father, and am the Firstborn (Doctrine and Covenants 93:21)

We leave it to the Church of Jesus Christ of Latter Day Saints to interpret what Smith meant by this. Although Mormon authorities may try to camouflage their interpretations when addressing non-Mormons, those who are well established in Mormonism know that the Church teaches that Jesus was the **literal** firstborn—the first among many spirit-beings that were begotten from Elohim and a heavenly mother. Angels like Lucifer, and men and women like us, are later spirit-children of Elohim. That is why Mormon Temple rites depict Jesus and Michael (brothers) commissioned by God to go forth and create for six days. Under the direction of the Twelve Apostles of the Mormon Church, Milton R. Hunter wrote the following.

The appointment of Jesus to be the Savior of the world was contested by one of the other sons of God. He was called Lucifer, son of the morning. Haughty, ambitious, and covetous of power and glory, this spirit-brother of Jesus desperately tried to become the Savior of mankind (The Gospel Through the Ages, p. 15)

Today's official Mormon interpretation of Joseph Smith's teaching concludes that Jesus is the first of many spirit-brothers. Brigham Young took Joseph Smith to mean that **Adam** was actually that God who begat Jehovah (Jesus) and his spirit-brothers (General Conference, April 9, 1852), but even though Brigham Young was closer to Joseph Smith than James E. Talmage and today's Mormon apostles and prophet, that extra step has been walked back. Even so, that Jesus (Jehovah) is an offspring of God (Elohim) is completely inconsistent with the Bible's presentation of the Person of Christ.

Although [Christ Jesus] existed in the form of God, [He] did not regard equality with God a thing to be grasped (Philippians 2:6)

For by Him all things were created, both in the heavens and on earth, visible and invisible, whether thrones or dominions or rulers or authorities—all things have been created through Him and for Him. He is before all things, and in Him all things hold together (Colossians 1:16)

When the Bible speaks of Jesus being "the firstborn of all creation" (Colossians 1:15), it is in this Colossians 1:16 sense. The Bible nowhere teaches that Jesus is a literal offspring of a heavenly father and his heavenly wife. The Greek word for "Firstborn" in Colossians 1:15 refers to Christ's preeminence—that He has the first place in everything. Jesus is not the brother of Lucifer. Jesus is Lucifer's Creator! "For by Him *all things* were created, both in the heavens and on earth, visible and invisible, *whether thrones or dominions or rulers or authorities—all things* have been created through Him and for Him." (Colossians 1:16). Correlated with Philippians 1:6, John 1:1, 14:9 and Hebrews 1:8, it is abundantly clear that Jesus is nothing less than the One True God.

Joseph Smith brings God the Father down to the level of an exalted man. He brings Jesus down to the level of Lucifer, a mere spirit-being born from Elohim. Having thus established a progression, he brings himself and his faithful followers up to the level of the gods (Elohim and Jehovah) that went before them. In the course of time and by certain works, it is said, they will progress and be exalted as gods over new worlds.

But such theologizing is the subject of the Deuteronomy 13:1-3 test! If any prophet or dreamer of dreams would have you go after other gods—those not consistent with the Bible's revelation of the One True God—then he is a deceiver and worthy of death. Are you willing to love God by rejecting the presumption of a prophet who denigrates God's unrivaled glory? God spoke through Moses thousands of years before Joseph Smith made his fantastic claims. God gave us the consistency test (Deuteronomy 13:1-3) for such a time as this.

CHAPTER 2

THE SECOND BIBLICAL TEST OF A PROPHET:
PREDICTIONS

DEUTERONOMY 18:20-22

Did any of Joseph Smith's predictive prophecies fail to come true? The question is not a matter of percentages, as if many correct predictions could overwhelm a failed one. Rather, God provided a simple test for our protection. If God genuinely speaks through a prophet, then nothing he predicts will ever be shown to have failed. Throughout history, those who claim such a direct line of communication with Almighty God as to call himself a "prophet" will inevitably resort to making definitive statements about the future, because the prophet seems to believe that God will surely make it come to pass. God, on the other hand, has told us to watch for His response to such things in the real unfolding of history in order to judge for ourselves whether or not the self-attesting prophet does genuinely speak for God. In the case of Joseph Smith, God does not step into history to bring Smith's predictions to pass. Even one example completely undermines Joseph Smith's claim of being a prophet.

Verily this is the word of the Lord, that the city New Jerusalem shall be built by the gathering of the saints, beginning at this place, even the place of the temple, which temple shall be reared in this generation...in this generation, upon the consecrated spot as I have appointed (Doctrines and Covenants 84:4,31)

Before testing Smith's prophecy, consider Jesus' prophecy about events to occur within a generation. Jesus said that "when you see all these things" (meaning the dozens of birth pangs predicted in preceding verses), then "*this generation* will not pass away" (Matthew 24:33-34) until His second coming takes place. Since the birth pangs have not yet even clearly begun, Jesus' prophecy is not yet testable. The generation that will see the birth pangs has not necessarily even arrived yet. However, His prophecy of the destruction of the Jewish Temple (Matthew 24:2) is now testable. It was proven true in 70 AD.

Joseph Smith's prophecy of a Temple he planned to build in Independence, Missouri within his lifetime is easily testable. All it would take for an American to test this prophecy is a road trip to Missouri, which many ex-Mormons have taken—to the detriment of their faith in Joseph Smith. The physical location of what was prophesied to be a soon-to-be-built Temple is pinpointed in D&C 84:3. It is the very spot where Smith stood. He clearly identified the place (D&C 84:31). The timeframe he gave, while speaking "the word of the Lord" (D&C 84:2,4) on behalf of none other than Jesus Christ (D&C 84:1) was within "this generation" (D&C 84:4, 31). But Smith did not anticipate the events that would keep him and his church from building their kingdom in Missouri. So, as that generation died off, Smith's prophecy failed and Smith himself was proven by the Deuteronomy 18:20-22 test to be a false prophet. No Temple was built on that spot in Missouri within that generation.

It is not difficult to prove that Joseph Smith failed the predictions test on multiple occasions. He prophesied the return of Christ by the year 1891 (History of the Church, vol. 2, p. 189). He predicted that the nations of the world would be dragged into the American Civil War (D&C 87:1-3). He foretold that the end-time signs in the skies will happen in "not many days" (D&C 88:87). All of these failed. But it is most essential that we understand the significance of the failed Independence, Missouri Temple prophecy.

There is a certain irony that God often employs in exposing false prophets. Muhammad prophesied that the Dajjal (Antichrist) would appear within seven months of the fall of Constantinople (Abu Dawud Book 37, Number 4281). Muslims did in fact conquer the capital of the Eastern Church in the fifteenth century, but no antichrist appeared within seven months. As a result, Muhammad himself was revealed for what he was—an antichrist (1 John 2:18,22-23). God used Muhammad's own failed antichrist prophecy to expose Muhammad's own antichrist spirit. God did similarly with Joseph Smith's Temple theology. God used Joseph Smith's own failed Temple prophecy to expose Joseph Smith's own antichrist Temple teachings.

Were Joseph Smith's teachings about the Temple very significant? A first-time reader of the Book of Mormon will be struck by its vast usage of Biblical language. In fact, Joseph Smith was pretty close to an orthodox Trinitarian when that first publication came out. But it was Smith's distinctives (mostly developed later in the Doctrine and Covenants, Pearl of Great Price, and non-canonical teachings) by which Smith was able to fashion himself as a unique Restorer of an apostate church, Prophet of God, Seer, and Revelator to be followed. His distinct contribution—the Church of Jesus Christ of Latter Day Saints—is largely a religion organized around teachings that relate to the Temple. The LDS Church claims Priesthood authority. Mormons conceive of themselves as having and conferring Aaronic and Melchizedekian Priesthoods. These distinctive claims relate to activities carried out in Mormon Temples.

The failure of Joseph Smith's Temple prophecy is not random; it is the failure of Joseph Smith's Temple theology itself. It is the failure of the Mormon claim to be the restored Church. It is the failure of Mormonism at the very point of its distinctive identity.

The Glory of the Temple in Jerusalem was it's revelation of the Person Jesus Christ. To miss this fulfillment and to try to reestablish Temple rites is an expression of a spirit of antichrist.

The Jerusalem Temple itself was only "a mere copy of the true one" (Hebrews 9:24). The true Temple is the place where God is. It is in heaven. The earthly representation was never the reality. The Jerusalem Temple was only made by human hands, a part of this creation (Hebrews 9:11). Aaronic Priests were descendants of Levi who served daily (Hebrews 9:6) in the Temple in Jerusalem offering bloody animal sacrifices that could only cover over sin for a time—never take sin away eternally. Once a year, one of them—the High Priest—went behind the veil entering "the holy place year by year with blood that is not his own" (Hebrews 9:25). The Temple and the Temple rites of the Aaronic Priesthood had one supreme purpose—to prophetically reveal the True Priest who can truly take away sin. They all pointed to Jesus, and they ended when He died. "Otherwise, He would have needed to suffer often since the foundation of the world; but now once at the consummation of the ages He has been manifested to put away sin by the sacrifice of

Himself" (Hebrews 9:26). This is the Gospel.

Mormon friend, since Joseph Smith's prophecy of a Missouri Temple failed, will you consider what the Bible teaches about the Melchizedekian Priesthood? It is not something that can be conferred upon any other man, because the entire point of it was the revelation of Jesus Christ as the Unique Priest who truly takes away sin. Genesis 14, Psalm 110, and Hebrews 7 will draw your attention away from earthly Temples, away from endowments, tokens, and your own authority, and focus your attention upon Jesus (see Appendix C: Who is of the Order of Melchizedek?).

Jesus is the Unique Priest described in Genesis 14:18-20, Psalm 110:4, and the Book of Hebrews. The question is whether you will receive the teachings of the Bible and thus honor Jesus Christ or confer upon yourself the authority that Joseph Smith claimed for himself. Who is the "priest forever according to the order of Melchizedek" (Psalm 110:4)? Is it the Lord Jesus, who alone put His own sacrificial blood on a wooden cross and a heavenly altar? Or is it the LDS President? Is it the Quorum of the Twelve? Is it the Seventy? Is it you?

Who are the Aaronic Priests? Are there many Aaronic Priests among the Mormons today? Or has Jesus Christ put an end to that Priesthood, it having accomplished its purpose in its time? "Now if perfection was through the Levitical priesthood (for on the basis of it the people received the Law), what further need was there for another priest to arise according to the order of Melchizedek, and not be designated according to the order of Aaron? For when the priesthood is changed, of necessity there takes place a change of law also" (Hebrews 7:11-12). Since the Bible says that priesthood changed—the Aaronic ending and giving way to Jesus' Melchizedekian Priesthood—how can you say that you are an Aaronic Priest?

Who would dare elevate himself to the highest place, where Jesus alone belongs (Philippians 2:9), and claim to be a priest of the order of Melchizedek? Did your Mormon leaders give their bodies as bread and their blood as wine to save you from your sins? Don't you see that the Bible sets apart Melchizedek for the expressed purpose (Hebrews 7) of setting all eyes on Jesus?

Joseph Smith's Temple-oriented non-gospel rebuilds the old Temple of the Law. It makes Temple rites, tokens, endowments, eternal marriages, baptism at the hands of certain men, laying on of the hands of certain men, and worthy living necessary Laws that must be obeyed in order to make it to the Father. The veil of the Temple was torn from top to bottom when Jesus died on the cross (Matthew 27:51), but the LDS "gospel" tries to sew it back together. It imagines God on the other side of the veil asking for certain handshakes and code words that the faithful learned on earth in a Mormon Temple. Human mediators provided these things, because according to Mormon theology, Christ Himself is not a sufficient Mediator. But listen to the Scriptures (1 Timothy 2:5).

The whole book of Galatians warns against so-called gospels that rebuild the Law, which is what Joseph Smith did when he rebuilt the Temple rituals. Galatians 1:6-9 tells us that such lies will falsely be called the Gospel of Christ. False gospels will enslave people under a system of self-righteousness (Galatians 4:9). They will catch people on a hamster wheel, prodding them to work hard to strive after a freedom that they can never attain (Galatians 5:3). All the while, they will deny and even mock the genuine Gospel of God's grace (Galatians 2:16). They will deride Christians who say that salvation is by grace alone through faith alone. Pointing to the sins they see in the lives of the Christians they know (Galatians 2:17), they will self-righteously assume themselves to have a better Gospel. But the genuine Gospel addresses all of this.

Salvation is by grace, even if we sometimes take it for granted.

For if I rebuild what I have once destroyed, I prove myself to be a transgressor. For through the Law I died to the Law, so that I might live to God. I have been crucified with Christ; and it is no longer I who lives, but Christ lives in me; and the life which I now live in the flesh I live by faith in the Son of God, who loved me and gave Himself up for me. I do not nullify the grace of God, for if righteousness comes through the Law, then Christ died needlessly (Galatians 2:18-21)

All the Temple requirements ended when God put them under the blood of Jesus. His blood poured over them and stopped our work.

When you were dead in your transgressions and the uncircumcision of your flesh, He made you alive together with Him, having forgiven us all our transgressions, having cancelled out the certificate of death consisting of decrees against us, which was hostile to us; and He has taken it out of the way, having nailed it to the cross (Colossians 2:13-14)

God doesn't save righteous people who first do what the LDS gospel demands.

He saved us, not on the basis of the deeds which we have done in righteousness, but according to His mercy, by the washing of regeneration and renewing by the Holy Spirit (Titus 3:5)

God hasn't yet saved those who are still boasting in their obedience to the Law.

For by grace you have been saved through faith; and that not of yourselves, it is the gift of God; not as a result of works, so that no one may boast (Ephesians 2:8-9)

God saves those who have come to trust completely in the imputed righteousness of Jesus Christ, recognizing themselves as being unrighteous.

But to the one who does not work, but believes in Him who justifies the ungodly, his faith is credited as righteousness (Romans 4:5)

Hating the Bible's Gospel of salvation—justification by faith alone—Joseph Smith did the unthinkable. He made his own translation of the Bible and literally added the word "not" into Romans 4:5! According to Smith, God does **not** justify the ungodly.

Who was Joseph Smith? According to Deuteronomy 18:20-22, if a self-attesting prophet makes even one prediction that fails, then he is not a genuine prophet. He does not speak for God. To speak under the pretense of the authority of Jesus Christ, while at the same time detracting from His glory, is to speak by an antichrist spirit. Rebuilding physical Temples and reinstituting Temple rites is to rebuild the Law and make men slaves to it. Jesus answers this folly. "Destroy this temple, and in three days I will raise it up" (John 2:19). The physical Temple was meant to reveal Jesus. He rose again three days after He died. No longer needed, the Temple building was torn down in 70 AD and was not raised up on the third day. Who is Joseph Smith to try to rebuild it? He said that he could, and prophesied thus (D&C 84), but he failed the prediction test. Likewise, anyone who attempts to establish their own righteousness via Mormon Temple rights will fail to attain God's righteousness, which comes only by grace through faith in the Jesus of the Bible.

CHAPTER 3

THE THIRD BIBLICAL TEST OF A PROPHET:
FRUIT

MATTHEW 7:15-17

Did Joseph Smith's character fail to offer him a clear endorsement? According to Jesus, the fruit of an alleged prophet's life will be obvious—one way or the other. False prophets were the subject of Jesus' warning, so like dates falling from a date tree, oranges from an orange tree, or apples from an apple tree, bad fruit falls from false prophets. Bad fruit will drop down from time to time. The man who picks it up to examine it will have to scratch his head. "I am really surprised that this would fall from him" the man will ponder. "I thought he was such a man of God. I hear he is a prophet. Would a prophet act like this?" Many people who see the bad fruit of the false prophet will go on believing in him anyway. Some people have an uncanny ability to live with cognitive dissonance. But Jesus commended the opposite. He Himself was never so angry as when He saw hypocrisy in the religious elite (Matthew 23). And he told us to test a prophet's fruit, not so that we could explain it away, but so that we could expose the kind of tree that makes that kind of fruit.

What are the fruits we need to look for? No matter who you look at (except Jesus Christ), if you put his life under a microscope, you are going to find sin. The Bible paints a pretty ugly picture of the nature of people (Romans 3). None of us would fair well if tested for sin. But in the Matthew 7:15-23 test, something more drastic and apparent is being spoken of. First of all, it is about false prophets who have wowed an audience (7:15, 22). Secondly, their actions don't match their words (7:15-16). Finally, there is no repentance for what is so obviously bad. So, look for self-aggrandizement, hypocrisy, and a lack of repentance.

King David was a true prophet who on a number of occasions fell into some profound sin. But David never even claimed for himself the status of being a prophet. He danced for an audience of One (2 Samuel 6:22). He didn't parade his great spirituality. Secondly, David's words (read the Psalms) matched his actions (read the historical narratives concerning him). Finally, read Psalm 51. Without the repentance we see there, David would have failed the Matthew 7 test.

The Bible contains a list of the fruits of the flesh in Galatians 5:19-21. If you see many or all of these fruits in a prophet you wish to test, and you also notice self-aggrandizement, hypocrisy, and a lack of repentance, then it is Biblically imperative that you acknowledge what is obvious. The clear fruit of his moral life exposes the false prophet for who he is. Such is the case with Joseph Smith.

Now the deeds of the flesh are evident, which are: immorality, impurity, sensuality, idolatry, sorcery, enmities, strife, jealousy, outbursts of anger, disputes, dissentions, factions, envying, drunkenness, carousing and things like these, of which I forewarn you, just as I have forewarned you, that those who practice such things will not inherit the kingdom of God (Galatians 5:19-21)

The first three marks of a flesh-driven man listed in Galatians— *immorality, impurity, and sensuality*—relate to sexual sin. The directive to ordinary Christians in Ephesians 5:3 is that there shouldn't even be a hint of sexual immorality associated with us. Should the standard be lowered for someone who claims to be a prophet of God? It should not. In fact, in order to test the fruit of a false prophet's life (as Jesus commanded in Matthew 7:15-23), there needs to be an obvious pattern that reveals a hidden identity. Tiger Woods was tarred and feathered by the media because of his sexual misconduct, but he never claimed to be a prophet. Joseph Smith was literally tarred and feathered when caught in adultery, but he nevertheless claims to be a prophet.

The instance for which Smith was tarred and feathered was part of an obvious pattern of sexual sin that reveals his hidden identity as a false prophet. His identity was marked by his own sin. LDS Sunday School resources will present Smith as an innocent victim. Certainly, the mob that attacked him in 1832 had no right to do what they did. But the Church Education Department will not mention Nancy Miranda Johnson. One of the reasons that Eli Johnson was so angry, and Dr. Dennison almost castrated Joseph, was the allegation that Joseph had been intimate with Eli's 16-year-old niece—Miranda Johnson. It was not the first allegation.

In addition to Nancy Miranda Johnson, there were allegations that Joseph Smith had sexual contact with Eliza Winters, Ms. Hill, Fanny Alger, and many others. Oliver Cowdery, whom the Introduction to the Book of Mormon cites as a key witness to its reliability, also witnesses to Joseph Smith's adultery! Emma Smith caught Joseph in a barn with Fanny Alger. In a letter dated January 21st, 1838, Oliver Cowdery called the incident "a dirty, nasty, filthy affair of his and Fanny Algers". But why take Oliver Cowdery's word for it? After all, the LDS church excommunicated Cowdery, in part for "seeking to destroy the character of Joseph Smith". Would it be enough if Emma Smith herself acknowledged what she saw? On August 28, 1847, in a long conversation with William McLellin, Emma Smith said the story was true (http://mormoncurtain.com/topic_emmasmith.html).

Regarding polygamy, none can deny (but many Mormons do not know) that Joseph Smith had at least 32 wives. According to Leviticus 18:18, "you shall not marry a woman in addition to her sister". But Joseph married Emily and Eliza Partridge—two sisters, and other sisters as well. Helen Mar Kimball was only 14 years old when Smith married her. Her journal indicates that she thought it was only to be a ceremonial marriage and she was very uncomfortable when it turned out that sex was expected of her. The others were usually 16 or older. In an effort to arrange a rendezvous with Sarah Ann Whitney, Smith wrote her a letter, in which he instructed her to burn it after reading. She did not burn it. It survives to this day and reveals the deceitful wickedness of the sex-crazed prophet.

The only thing to be careful of is to find out when Emma comes, then you cannot be safe but when she is not here, then there is the most perfect safety…Only be careful to escape observation, as much as possible. I know it is a heroic undertaking; but so much the greater friendship and the more joy; when I see you I will tell you all my plans. I cannot write them on paper. Burn this letter as soon as you read it; keep it all locked up in your breasts, my life depends upon it…I close my letter, I think Emma won't come tonight. If she don't, don't fail to come tonight. I subscribe myself your most obedient, and affectionate, companion and friend. Joseph Smith (Joseph

Smith, Jr to Newell K. Whitney, Elizabeth Ann Whitney, etc 18 August 1842, George Albert Smith Family Papers, Special Collections, Marriott Library, University of Utah, Salt Lake City, Utah, text and signature of this document in the handwriting of Joseph Smith, Jr.)

That Joseph Smith tried to reintroduce polygamy when even worldly society has progressed beyond it is an astonishingly simple proof that he was no prophet of God. But Joseph Smith's sexual misconduct wasn't even confined to plural marriage. The so-called revelations that he received came after his immorality and were an obvious attempt to self-justify. Smith was not like King David who fell into adultery. David repented in Psalm 51. But Smith self justified in D&C 132. David lived in a time when God was overlooking polygamy. Joseph lived in a time when even secular folk knew that polygamy was wrong. David was a man after God's own heart. Joseph was a man after the deeds of the flesh.

Sorcery is next in the list of deeds of the flesh found in the fifth chapter of Galatians. As rare as it is that someone would practice outright sorcery, Joseph Smith is clearly guilty of doing so. He used his top hat as a magical conduit when dictating the words of the Book of Mormon. The witnesses to his supposed translation acknowledge that Smith wasn't even looking at gold plates as he told them what to write. His face was buried in his hat from whence came the words he recited. Additionally, Smith died with an occult item—a Jupiter Talisman—in his pocket. What's more, the handshakes and rituals of the Temple rites that Smith borrowed from Masonry are from the occult. Which prophet in the Bible could be credibly accused of sorcery? But this fruit falls from the kind of tree that produces it.

The next eight fruits—*enmities, strife, jealousy, outbursts of anger, disputes, dissentions, factions, and envying*—also describe Joseph Smith well. Read the sermon Smith preached at Elder King Follett's funeral. It is where Smith most clearly lays out his aberrant theology. But notice how contentious Smith is. One would hardly think that a funeral would be the time and place to pronounce 99% of Christian ministers to be false prophets, but that is what Smith does. Why would the name Alexander Campbell come up? Could it be that Campbell was a restorationist before Smith was, a lot of Smith's people were Campbellites before deserting to Smith, and the two leaders were bitter rivals? Read Joseph Smith's childish response to the book review that Alexander Campbell wrote on the Book of Mormon. Interestingly, Alexander Campbell pegged many of the problems with the supposed revelation as early as 1931. But the *enmity, strife, jealousy, outbursts of anger, disputes, dissentions, factions, and envying* between the two ministers over the years was palpable.

The Biblical list of these fruits of the flesh not only describe Joseph Smith's interactions with Alexander Campbell and other professing Christian ministers, it describes his relationship with virtually anyone and everyone else who didn't follow him as a prophet. The honest Mormon will not settle with the trite cop out that labels everything as "persecution".

There was always a reason why Joseph Smith ended up in jail. In New York, he was a con artist, falsely alleging his ability to recover buried treasure. His defense in that hearing was not to hedge his bet, saying he never made such claims. Rather, he said that his seer stones and hat trick really do work, but the treasure keeps on running away just before he recovers it. In Ohio, Joseph Smith didn't just get run out of town because of his strange teachings. Rather, he tried to start a bank. He deceived people about how much money they had in reserve. His scheme collapsed and he fled. In Illinois, he burnt down a printing press who wrote things about him that he didn't like! Quite simply, everywhere he went, Joseph Smith was clearly characterized by *enmities, strife, jealousy, outbursts of anger, disputes, dissentions, factions, and envying.*

The Biblical list in Galatians 5 is not exhaustive. It also includes *drunkenness, carousing and things like these.* What else characterized the life of Joseph Smith need not be mentioned. A clear pattern of obviously bad fruit is apparent to anyone who is willing to investigate the history of his life without looking through the lens of blind devotion. Speaking of blind devotion, remember that the entire point of Jesus' Divine instruction in Matthew 7:15-23 and John's inspired instruction in 1 John 4:1 is that we test alleged prophets *objectively.* If prior to testing him, one were to conclude already that Smith must be a prophet, that presupposition kind of defeats the purpose. One shouldn't heed the prophets words until *after* it becomes obvious that his life passes God's tests.

Anyone who has such a pattern of sexual immorality, such a history of divisiveness, and such participation in the occult is a false prophet. He did not repent of these things, but built a "church" upon them. With regard to his sexual immorality, it gave rise to the Warren Jeffs of the world. With regard to his divisiveness, it gave rise to the worst slaughter of innocent travelers in America's history—the Mountain Meadows

Massacre. With regard to his sorcery, it gave rise to Mormon Temple Rites, by which many thousands are deceived into thinking they are attaining to the Celestial Kingdom even as they descend into occultism.

Jesus was concerned to protect us, so He pointed to something obvious that would expose something hidden. False prophets may have amazing abilities that hide their true identity. They may prophesy, cast out demons, and perform miracles, but this is not proof that they belong to Christ. The obvious sign that reveals the hidden identity of false prophets is when their sins find them out.

CHAPTER 4

THE FOURTH BIBLICAL TEST OF A PROPHET:
MIRACLES

DEUTERONOMY 34:10-12, JOHN 14:11

Moses brought a major change to the economy under which humans needed to relate to God. God proved Moses a prophet by the miracles He provided. Jesus brought a major change to that which existed from the time of Moses. God proved Jesus a prophet (and more than a prophet) by the miracles He provided. Joseph Smith claimed that we have entered into the latter days and that God has now restored Priesthood authority and the true visible church. Did God prove Joseph Smith a prophet by miracles provided?

Prior to answering that question, it is essential to give examples of what constitutes a miraculous validation of a prophet. Muslims say that the Qur'an is a miracle because it is just too beautiful, too meaningful, and too influential in the world to have come from an ordinary illiterate man. But those of us who are not impressed by its sound, fury, or the effect it has upon the world will not acknowledge the "miracle". Genuine "signs and wonders" ought to be big enough to warrant the names. A sign must be clear enough that it points to God. A wonder must be amazing enough that it leaves the observer without any good explanation apart from having seen the work of the hand of God.

The miracles associated with the ministry of Moses were signs and wonders. Each of the ten plagues told the world that the God of Israel is superior to the god of the Nile and the various gods of the Egyptians. The parting of the Red Sea to allow the escape of God's people was so big that the world has never stopped talking about it. When God instituted the Law of Moses, including the Ten Commandments that Moses brought down from the mountain, no Israelite had any excuse if he didn't believe.

The miracles associated with the ministry of Jesus even surpassed the signs and wonders that validated Moses. The last verses of the last of the five books of Moses anticipated that this would be so. In accordance with Deuteronomy 34:10-12 and Deuteronomy 18:15-19, a Greater Prophet had arrived and humanity was accountable to listen to every word that would fall from His lips.

Jesus came to fulfill the Law of Moses (Matthew 5:17) and bring certain changes to the economy under which people related to God. All animal sacrifices would stop at the cross. Dietary codes were stopped. Sabbath rest changed from Saturday stillness to the perpetual rest that believers find in Christ (Hebrews 4). Salvation would forevermore come by calling on the Name of Jesus (Acts 4:12). Surely God would not change so much without giving us reason to trust the Prophet.

According to Jesus, we are to "believe because of the works themselves" (John 14:11). Jesus opened the eyes of the blind, restored hearing to the deaf, healed lepers, caused those who were lame from birth to pick up their mat and walk home. Jesus raised the dead! Jesus did not need to part a Sea to cross over it. He could walk on water! Jesus could face a hurricane on the Sea and make it completely calm with the simple command, "Be still" (Mark 4:39). Jesus turned water into wine. He cast out demons. He did many miracles, including healing everyone present who had any need of healing (Matthew 4:23).

Jesus also prophesied. He spoke a New Covenant to supersede the old. It was a monumental change. How then could we trust that this Prophet really was from God? After instituting a New Covenant in His blood (Matthew 26:28), He proved it by rising from the dead (1 Corinthians 15)! Because of the undeniable signs and wonders that the Lord performed, especially His own resurrection from the dead, all men are responsible to repent and believe in Him (Acts 17:30).

Moses and Jesus brought massive changes to the order of the spiritual universe. We can see what made Jesus greater than Moses, so we can understand His authority to change things that prevailed before. When Peter stood up to preach, he started to speak of Jesus by appealing to His miracles.

"Men of Israel, listen to these words: Jesus the Nazarene, a man attested to you by God with miracles and wonders and signs which God performed through Him in your midst, just as you yourselves know..." (Acts 2:22)

But was Joseph Smith accredited by clear signs and wonders? Even if he had done a few, that would not be proof enough for those who believe the Bible, since the Bible provides at least the six other tests applied in this book. Jesus warned us that when the latter days truly arrive in their fullness "false Christs and false prophets will arise and will show great signs and wonders, so as to mislead, if possible, even the elect" (Matthew 24:24). That is how clear the miracles of the last lying prophets will be. But Joseph Smith didn't even have miracles that were objectively supernatural. His "prophetic" utterances sought to change everything (ie all the churches are wrong, the LDS Church has a restored Priesthood authority, God was once a man, salvation is by grace only after all that we can do, Temple rites, etc). But he had precious few examples of any miracles. Alexander Campbell, in 1831, mentioned that there was no lack of trying for miracles among Smith and his inner circle, but miracles simply weren't occurring.

The greatest miracle that Joseph Smith allegedly performed was recovering gold plates from Moroni and translating them from Reformed Egyptian, a language Smith didn't know. But the supposed witnesses to such a thing have not given reliable testimony. Oliver Cowdery, David Whitmer and Martin Harris may have held to their testimony in some respects, but they left Smith and the LDS church after later "miraculous revelations" came along. When you study the eight witnesses (certain among Smith's family and friends), they actually saw very little. Not only so, the big three later admitted to seeing the plates "with spiritual eyes", not physical eyes.

If any of the 11 "witnesses" did see or lift some plates, they did not examine them to see if they looked authentic. Even assuming that "Reformed Egyptian" is a highly efficient tongue, the Book of Mormon requires more than 500 pages when translated into English using a 7" by 5" page, 10-point font, single spaced. Since 1 cubic foot of gold weighs 1,206 pounds, can you imagine how many tons of gold would have been required to house 500 pages worth of material? There is a reason why metal has never in the history of the world been used to hold inscriptions of vast amounts of information. Yet Nephi and company were supposedly running around with long books, carrying inscribed metal as if it were papyrus marked with ink. What mighty men they were! Joseph Smith's not-too-critical 8 witnesses reported that they "hefted the plates". But the plates were covered when they lifted them, and being in a posture of "faith", they did not ask hard questions about how so long a book would be contained on an amount of metal that weighed so little that it could be hefted.

That they would have lifted less than a hundred pounds of metal is actually evidence that whatever was under that blanket was not Moroni's plates, because less than 100 pounds of metal couldn't contain even First Nephi, let alone the exceedingly long books like Mosiah and Alma. Of course, one could argue that one letter in Reformed Egyptian contains an entire page worth of information when translated into English. But if that kind of supernatural explaining is required then we are no longer talking about evidence. We are merely back to a faith statement, and the point is established that whatever the 11 witnesses saw does not meet the definition of a miracle. Once again, they only saw with the "eyes of faith" and the public wasn't allowed to see anything.

There was nothing miraculous about what little they actually saw. As to translation, since Smith simply buried his head in his hat and claimed to see things, there was no miraculous demonstration at all. The Book of Mormon is simply what Smith claimed he translated. But there is no guarantor that his translation was anything but the creation of his own mind.

The second greatest alleged miracle of Smith's life was the supposed visit he received from the Father and the Son when he was about 16 years old. It was during this supposed visit in 1820 that God told Joseph that none of the churches were true. The problem here is that Smith's own earliest written account of the event disagrees with the story (http://www.mrm.org/first-vision)! In 1832, Smith mentions only one personage appearing. Nine differing versions of the story would appear over the years, the current LDS orthodox version not appearing until 1840.

In Lesson 21 of Primary 5: Doctrine and Covenants and Church History, the LDS Church states as if it was a matter of fact that "Ezra Booth joined the Church in 1831 after seeing the Prophet heal Elsa Johnson's arm". But evidently Ezra Booth wasn't all that blown away by what he saw. After seeing more of Joseph Smith and his church, he concluded that Smith was a fraud.

The miracles test requires sober judgment. Are we to believe that God allowed Moses' words in the Old Testament and Jesus' words in the New Testament to be corrupted? Consider the power God revealed from heaven to validate these prophets. Yet here we have one Joseph Smith claiming that he has provided the most correct book in all the world! And what is the guarantee of this claim, such that men ought to be held accountable to believing this revelation? Did Smith walk on water, open blind eyes, raise the dead? If Jesus needed to have greater miracles than Moses to demonstrate supersession (Deuteronomy 34:10-12), then has Joseph Smith performed greater miracles than Jesus in order that we ought to believe that his books supersede the Christian Bible?

Mormons will hold up the King James Bible and affirm that they believe it too, but where their Scriptures abrogate what was written before (Ephesians 2:8-9, Hebrews 7-9, Romans 4:5, Galatians, etc), they presume errors in the "translation" of the Bible. When it comes down to it, they believe Smith over the Bible. The fourth test simply asks: Where are the miracles, signs, and wonders? Jesus performed His miracles "in the midst" of the general population, so the Apostles could remind the people what they saw with their own eyes. Peter appealed to what the whole nation of Israel had seen—"just as you yourselves know" (Acts 4:22). What miracles did Joseph Smith show the nation?

CHAPTER 5

THE FIFTH BIBLICAL TEST OF A PROPHET:
MEASURES

MATTHEW 7:1-2

After four chapters, we have already tested Joseph Smith by four Biblical measures. Smith failed the Deuteronomy 13 **consistency** test because his view of a progressing Elohim and others progressing to become Gods is a direct contradiction to passages like Isaiah 43:10, Malachi 3:6 and Mark 12:29. Smith failed the Deuteronomy 18 **predictions** test because he spoke in the Name of the Lord in D&C 84 but no Temple was completed in Independence, MO "in this generation". Smith failed the Matthew 7 **fruit** test because his sexual immorality, sorcery, divisiveness, self-aggrandizement, hypocrisy, and lack of repentance were evident signs of his hidden identity. Smith failed the Deuteronomy 34:10-12 **miracles** test because the supposed signs that accompanied his ministry were spurious and amounted to nothing compared to those that testified to the authenticity of Moses and Jesus, whom Smith allegedly supersedes.

Despite what the Biblical tests are showing, many if not most Mormons who have read this far will still be convinced that Smith was a genuine prophet. How is that possible? My introductory comments focused on the Introduction to the Book of Mormon and exposed where it diverges into aberrant epistemological foundations. If the memory of subjective experiences is one's final arbiter of truth, then what the Bible says doesn't ultimately matter. But Matthew 7:1-2 anticipated that sinful man would often employ faulty scales in weighing truth claims. So, the very measures that one employs to validate a truth claim will often turn around and invalidate that claim in the end. This is the case with those who validate Joseph Smith by the scale of personal experiences. Even with this faulty scale, personal experiences do not tip the balance in favor of Joseph Smith.

The human heart and/or the devil can give the strongest impressions that everything in the Book of Mormon and the entire system of the LDS Church are true. But how can Mormons explain those who have experienced profound testimonies confirming it all to be true—only to later experience something even more profound that confirms the opposite?

When Lynn Wilder received the "burning in the bosom" she testified to it in front of the Church. Her tears flowed like rain as she delighted in what God had confirmed to her. She and her husband remained faithful Mormons for years. He became a High Priest. She became a Professor at BYU. They raised their kids in the LDS Church.

Their son Micah excelled as a young Mormon like Saul of Tarsus excelled as a young Pharisee (Philippians 3:4-6). He was the youngest person ever to get a position in the Temple in Salt Lake City. He used to do baptisms for the dead before the sun came up. He went on mission to Orlando determined to win the city. But God.

But now apart from the Law the righteousness of God has been manifested, being witnessed by the Law and the Prophets, even the righteousness of God through faith in Jesus Christ for all those who believe; for there is no distinction; for all have sinned and fall short of the glory of God, being justified as a gift by His grace through the redemption which is in Christ Jesus (Romans 3:21-24)

The gospel of God's grace met Micah Wilder in Orlando. His father and his mother (the BYU Professor) as well as many family and friends also experienced the grace of God shortly thereafter. Now tears flow as they testify about the grace of God. You can watch Micah's new testimony online by searching for Adam's Road Band. As you do, consider that their testimony about the current gospel came after their "burning in the bosom" experience with the Mormon church. The later experience accounts for the earlier experience, but the earlier experience cannot account for the later.

If subjective personal experiences were really the test for truth, then even this test would testify strongly against the Mormon church! Matthew 7:1-2 comes back to bite Joseph Smith. He claimed that all the churches were wrong. Smith was therefore very judgmental of the Body of Christ. The measure he used was not the Word of God but an appeal to personal experience. Yet by that measure, the Body of Christ worldwide pronounces a right judgment back upon Smith. We have had nearly 200 years to consider his claim and only 15 million people on a planet of 6 billion are affirming it. The LDS church is not even keeping up with worldwide population growth (remember that its been 200 years since the latter days supposedly began). In fact, if the number of Mormons who stopped attending services were dropped from the count, then the LDS Church is in numerical decline. The subjective testimony of almost everyone alive today (more than 99% of the people in the world) is that Joseph Smith was a false prophet.

I for one have read the Book of Mormon and feel completely confirmed that it is a fraud from the mind of Joseph Smith. Of course, the argument goes that one must sincerely seek to believe. But it is circular reasoning to say that I must have any measure of faith in the Book of Mormon in order for God to confirm to my spirit that He is the ultimate Author of the Book of Mormon. I already have a certain faith in the God of the Bible. The Bible already provided me with the Gospel. God gave no indication that He would lose the Gospel after the death of John the Apostle and recover it at the arrival of Joseph Smith. On the contrary, He warned time and again about the appearance of men like Joseph Smith who would try to change it (Matthew 7:15-20, Mark 7:7-8, Luke 11:52, John 10:11-13, Acts 20:28-31, Romans 16:17-19, 1 Corinthians 14:36-38, 2 Corinthians 11:3-6, Galatians 1:6-10, Ephesians 4:14-16, Philippians 3:15-20, Colossians 2:8, 1 Thessalonians 5:21, 2 Thessalonians 2:2, 1 Timothy 4:1-2, 2 Timothy 4:1-5, Titus 1:9, Hebrews 2:1, 12:15, 13:9, James 5:19-20, 1 Peter 3:15, 2 Peter 2:1, 1 John 4:1, 2 John 7, 3 John 9, Jude 3, Revelation 2:2,14,20, 3:9).

There is a question that every Mormon needs to answer. Who gets to say what is true? If God gets to tell us what is true, then surely the tests of a prophet He provided in His Book need to be applied to Joseph Smith. But if someone insists on clinging to a testimony of what God allegedly spoke privately in his or her heart, then surely that person considers himself or herself to be a god. If that is you, then you ultimately trust in yourself to determine what is true. Mormonism will teach you that your intelligence is eternal. If that were true, then you would be God (a part of you would have no beginning, even as God has no beginning). But if that is the lie of the devil, and Genesis 3:5 exposes that it is, then your profound emotional experience likewise came from him and the desires of your own flesh.

The Book of Mormon was "a delight to the eyes" and "desirable to make one wise" (Genesis 3:5), so you took and ate of it without properly checking it against what God had already spoken (Genesis 2:17). It was enough for you that what the Serpent said was very similar to what God said in the Bible. But for all of the similarities between what Joseph Smith says in the Book of Mormon and what God says in the Bible, Smith gets it twisted. God never said "you shall not eat from any tree of the garden" (Genesis 3:1). Satan said that. God never said "to ponder in their hearts the message it contains, and then to ask God, the Eternal Father, in the name of Christ if the book is true." Joseph Smith said that. James 1:5 instructs us to ask for wisdom, but Proverbs 2 tells us how God will answer. God imparts wisdom through His Word.

Beloved, do not believe every spirit, but test the spirits to see whether they are from God, because many false prophets have gone out into the world. (1 John 4:1)

How do we test? We test by God's Word—Deuteronomy 13, Deuteronomy 18, Matthew 7, Deuteronomy 34, Titus 1. The chapters of this book have already tested Joseph Smith by these passages. Two of the most powerful tests remain to be employed. For the sake of your own soul, please stop trusting yourself as the ultimate decider of truth. Trust in the only true God as you test the facts relating to Joseph Smith. Let the Bible (the last two tests come from John 3:12 and Mark 10:45) test the prophet.

CHAPTER 6

THE SIXTH BIBLICAL TEST OF A PROPHET: **ACCURACY**

JOHN 3:12

The sixth test is not subjective. It is an objective way to test an aspiring prophet. It in no way depends upon wishful thinking or emotions in the private chambers of the human heart. It simply depends on truth. It assumes a correspondence view of truth, which is nothing more than the mere acknowledgement that if something is true, then it corresponds to reality as it actually is. Jesus was capable of disclosing a myriad of mysteries of heaven that we currently know nothing about. He chose to tell us only what He did tell us. He told Nicodemus, "If I told you earthly things and you do not believe, how will you believe if I tell you heavenly things" (John 3:12). Although Jesus didn't tell all, all that He told was true. Had He proven to be inaccurate concerning the earthly things of which He spoke, then He would not have been a truthful prophet and there would be no sense in listening to anything He might say about heavenly things. If anyone who claims to be a prophet is in demonstrable error about things that can be tested, then we should not trust his non-testable assertions about heavenly things. The so-called prophet fails the accuracy test.

Joseph Smith bought an old Egyptian papyrus and four mummies from a sketchy salesman named Michael Chandler. Since Smith had long asserted that he was a "seer" (see Mosiah 8:15), he and his church were eager to see if Joseph could translate the Egyptian papyrus. Smith recorded in his personal journal how God was helping him unlock the meaning of the Egyptian hieroglyphics. He proceeded to "translate" the Book of Abraham, which is now canonized by the Mormon Church in the Pearl of Great Price. Now, here was something that could be tested.

Joseph Smith's earlier work—the Book of Mormon—was not testable, because Smith was allegedly instructed to return the golden plates to the angel. The world was left to take or leave Joseph Smith's word for it. At the time that Smith undertook the project to translate the Egyptian papyrus, no one on the American continent had a knowledge of Egyptian hieroglyphics, but at least there was some physical thing that could potentially be tested one day. Smith probably never foresaw that academic discipline known as Egyptology arising, but today, the day of testing has arrived.

When the Rosetta Stone was discovered in 1799, which had Egyptian hieroglyphics in juxtaposition to parallel texts in known languages, linguists in Europe began to unlock the meaning of Egyptian hieroglyphics. Now that certain scholars (Egyptologists) can translate Michael Chandler's artifact, the Book of Abraham can be tested. The leading scholars in the field tell us that the artifact relates the story of an Egyptian funeral rite. It makes no mention of Abraham. It is not in any way, shape or form what Joseph Smith said it was. The drawings he completed and included as facsimiles in the Pearl of Great Price were not consistent with the actual characters depicted on the papyrus. In other words, Smith made up the Book of Abraham and called it a translation of the document the church bought from Michael Chandler. The Church has the papyrus in their possession (it was not destroyed in the Chicago Fire and what they have is what Smith had). If they tell us earthly things that cannot be trusted, how can we trust them when they tell us heavenly things?

We move on to a second area of Joseph Smith's teaching that *can* be tested. There is a stunning lack of archeological evidence for the existence of the peoples that the Book of Mormon places on the North American continent. Discoveries of impressive ruins in and around Guatemala led many Mormons to want to affix the location of the Book of Mormon to that region. But the Book of Mormon speaks definitively of the Hill Cumorah in New York. It references the area from there to the Rocky Mountains. Joseph Smith would prophesy about bones of people they discovered in Illinois, even telling the supposed name of the deceased "Lamanite". It's easy to say that the events of the Book of

Mormon really took place on some tiny sliver of land in Meso-America that has yet to be definitively located. Such a claim isn't testable. But Joseph Smith knew where he was talking about (see the Youtube video "Joseph Knew" by Rod Meldrum). The LDS Church has a welcome center on Cumorah, but why don't they simply unearth the artifacts from the supposed 2-million-man battle that happened there? The archeological proofs for the events that happened in the Old and New Testament are remarkable, but the evidence for the Book of Mormon is missing.

A final test of Joseph Smith's accuracy that I will mention is the Kinderhook Plates, produced near Kinderhook, Illinois. Smith's claim to be able to interpret tongues and produce "a volume of holy scripture comparable to the Bible" left some people wanting to know if such a claim were true. So two men hammered some Chinese-looking characters onto six small bell-shaped brass plates. They tried to make them look as ancient and authentic as possible. Then they took these plates to the prophet.

Not discerning the spirits of the tricksters, Joseph Smith took the plates (made up some exciting origin for them) and set his hand to the work of translating. How far he got, I do not know, but he evidently "knew" that he was hearing from God.

No one can know what was going on inside of the head of Joseph Smith. Was he deluded? Was he aware that he was making stuff up, or did he genuinely think that he was hearing from God? No one can crawl around inside the head of another, and God never asked us to do so. He did however ask us to test the spirits (1 John 4:1). To do so doesn't always require the spiritual gift of discerning spirits (1 Corinthians 12:10). Sometimes it only requires that we look at what is easily testable and decide not to believe those whose testable statements prove false. Wilbur Fugate, one of the originators of the Kinderhook Plate fraud, eventually made his ploy known. He broadcast to the world that he made the plates in order to test Joseph Smith.

It is not as if Smith looked at those plates and simply said what I would have said, "I have no idea what those things are". Rather, he leaped at the chance to bring forth yet another confirmation that his Book of Mormon is "comparable to the Bible". He said he knew to whom the plates belonged—"a descendant of Ham, through the loins of Pharaoh, King of Egpyt" (Joseph Smith, History of the Church, V. 5, p. 372). Joseph Smith didn't think that such a claim could really be tested.

But then, he didn't know Wilbur Fugate had duped him. Neither did Smith know that modern science would one day be able to test the age of the plates. In 1980 scientists tested one and proved that it came from modern times. So, Wilbur Fugate wasn't the only one making stuff up.

If Joseph Smith tells us earthly things and we do not believe him, how can we believe him if he tells us heavenly things? Smith told us that he literally translated the Book of Abraham right off of the Egyptian papyrus that the Church purchased from Michael Chandler for $2,400. At josephsmithpapers.org, the LDS church displays the July 6, 1835 certificate that Chandler provided. If God desired to validate Joseph Smith in any way, then wouldn't something in the actual Egyptian Papyrus from which Smith translated at least mention Abraham? Wouldn't a non-Mormon Egyptologist be willing to verify that the Book of Abraham and the actual Papyrus have anything to do with each other whatsoever? Wouldn't there be plenty of archeological evidence for the Book of Mormon right here in North America? Wouldn't the Kinderhook Plates have something in common with the fantastical claims that Smith made about them?

God is not a deceiver! He is not trying to trick people. He is not honored by stretching someone's faith to the point where one is forced to hate the truth. Rather, He is a consistent God and delights in peace (1 Corinthians 14:33). He is not the author of confusion. He rejoices in the truth and imparts a sound mind. If an alleged prophet fails in the testable things he says, then we should not trust anything he says, especially when he claims to reveal the mysteries of heaven.

CHAPTER 7

THE SEVENTH BIBLICAL TEST OF A PROPHET:
MOTIVES

MARK 10:45

Did Joseph Smith leave evidence of an unholy agenda? When Jesus was taken prisoner, he went like a lamb to the slaughter. He rebuked Peter for drawing the sword. Jesus put up no fight. The cross that awaited Him was the worst thing for His flesh, yet He willingly allowed Himself to be taken there. What motivated Him?

For even the Son of Man did not come to be served, but to serve, and to give His life a ransom for many (Mark 10:45).

Joseph Smith, on the other hand, betrayed some very self-serving motives in the exercise of his alleged prophetic gift. Paul paused in the middle of his teaching about spiritual gifts (1 Corinthians 12-14) to bring us a beautiful description of what must always remain the motive behind them (1 Corinthians 13). "Love does not seek its own", but Joseph Smith's alleged prophecies too often worked to the benefit of his own flesh. A pattern of all-too-convenient prophecies betray the motives of the man behind them.

Before looking at an obvious example in the life of Joseph Smith, consider that Muhammad pulled the same move 1,200 years earlier. He took plural wives. The stronger ones (Hafsa and Aisha) got jealous and angry about his time with another (Mary the Copt). Muhammad was on the ropes. So he dropped a prophetic bomb on them. By dropping Surah 66, Muhammad was all-too-conveniently freed to sleep with whichever wives he wanted to sleep with. Hafsa and Aisha were warned that if they don't straighten up, then they'll be replaced and wind up in hell (alongside Noah's wife, according to the prophet). Compare Muhammad's tactic to what Joseph Smith did.

And let mine handmaid, Emma Smith, receive all those that have been given unto my servant Joseph, and who are virtuous and pure before me; and those who are not pure, and have said they were pure, shall be destroyed, saith the Lord God. For I am the Lord thy God, and ye shall obey my voice; and I give unto my servant Joseph that he shall be made ruler over many things; for he hath been faithful over a few things, and from henceforth I will strengthen him. And I command mine handmaid, Emma Smith, to abide and cleave unto my servant Joseph, and to none else. But if she will not abide this commandment she shall be destroyed, saith the Lord; for I am the Lord thy God, and will destroy her if she abide not in my law. But if she will not abide this commandment, then shall my servant Joseph do all things for her, even as he hath said; and I will bless him and multiply him and give unto him an hundred-fold in this world, of fathers and mothers, brothers and sisters, houses and lands, wives and children, and crowns of eternal lives in the eternal worlds. And again, verily I say, let mine handmaid forgive my servant Joseph his trespasses; and then shall she be forgiven her trespasses, wherein she has trespassed against me; and I, the Lord thy God, will bless her, and multiply her, and make her heart to rejoice. (Doctrine and Covenants 132:52-56)

Muslims think that the burning in their bosom that they feel when they read the Qur'an is all the evidence they need. If only they could open their eyes to see 1 Corinthians 13 and compare it to Surah 66. Then the beauty of genuine love would expose the lie of self-serving control tactics. The same goes for D&C 132:54-55. Are there any similarities between it and Surah 66:5?

Perhaps his Lord, if he divorced you [all], would substitute for him wives better than you—submitting [to Allah], believing, devoutly obedient, repentant, worshipping, and traveling—[ones] previously married and virgins (Surah 66:5)

…But if she will not abide this commandment she shall be destroyed…and I will bless him and multiply him and give unto him an hundred-fold in this world…houses and lands, wives and children, and crowns of eternal lives in the eternal worlds (Doctrine and Covenants 132:54-55)

In both cases, the prophet threatens the wife. Hafsa, Aisha and Emma Smith need to understand that if they don't accept the prophet's other wives, then they "shall be destroyed" (D&C 132:4) and "enter the fire with those who enter" (Surah 66:10), just like "the wife of Noah and the wife of Lot" (66:10). After all, that's what happens to prophet's wives when they won't submit. But how will that affect the prophet?

It's no skin off the prophet's nose! If she chooses not to go along with plural marriages, then she needs to understand that she is easily replaceable! Allah is going to "substitute for him wives better than you" (Surah 66:5). Do you think it is hard for Elohim to "multiply him and give unto him an hundred-fold in this world...houses and lands, wives and children" (D&C 132:55)? God will replace you a hundred times over.

There is a simple and obvious question that needs to be asked. Do these supposed prophecies meet the definition of love given in 1 Corinthians 13 that must attend genuine prophecies, or do these supposed prophecies betray the self-serving motives of someone who speaks presumptuously in the name of the Lord? These "prophecies" address a particular man's personal marital conflict. They are obvious tactics of husbands using prophetic rhetoric to control their wives. Joseph Smith has this fantastic ability to speak in the name of the Lord, which like a card in his back pocket, he can pull out when he really needs to get his way.

And now, as pertaining to this law, verily, verily, I say unto you, I will reveal more unto you, hereafter; therefore, let this suffice for the present. Behold, I am Alpha and Omega. Amen. (Doctrine and Covenants 132:66)

Insert card back into pocket for future use. It is astonishing that Joseph Smith signs off as if God Himself—Alpha and Omega—has just revealed plural marriages for time and eternity, given Joseph Smith unprecedented authority, and threatened Joseph's poor wife in a revelation that will last—like the Bible—for time and eternity. Poor Emma Smith has been dead and gone for more than a hundred years now. She's off to populate a world with Joseph, so does she really need her humiliation recorded in Scripture forevermore? Or was Joseph Smith simply prophesying falsely for his own particular situation? 1 Corinthians 13 will enlighten those who do not harden their hearts.

If I speak with the tongues of men and of angels, but do not have love, I have become a noisy gong or a clanging cymbal. If I have the gift of prophecy, and know all mysteries and all knowledge...but do not have love, I am nothing. Love is patient, love is kind and is not jealous; love does not brag and is not arrogant, does not act unbecomingly; it does not seek its own, is not provoked, does not take into account a wrong suffered, does not rejoice in unrighteousness, but rejoices with the truth; bears all things, believes all things, hopes all things, endures all things. Love never fails...But now faith, hope, love, abide these three; but the greatest of these is love (1 Corinthians 13)

Joseph Smith failed to love Emma in D&C 132, so it is clearly not a prophecy from God. The motives of Joseph's heart rise to the surface when D&C 132 is read objectively—without the lens of preconceived devotion. Joseph Smith was not fully devoted to Emma Smith. Otherwise, there would never have been the incident in the barn with Fanny Alger. He wouldn't have been smitten by Sarah Pratt and asked for her to be "one of his spiritual wives, for the Lord had given her to him as a special favor for his faithfulness" (Article "Sarah M. Pratt" by Richard A. Van Wagoner, Dialogue, Vol.19, No.2, p.72). She said no. It is evident that Joseph Smith tried to use prophecy as a tool to get his way.

Smith drops prophecies to add authority to his own words. He wants the absolute obedience that ought to accompany a "verily, verily, I say unto you" (132:66) from God. But isn't this motive obvious?

First of all, why would God be speaking in the Middle English of the 1600s if it were really Him bringing new revelation in 1843 America? Could it be that Joseph Smith was trying to make His lyrics sound as impressive as the King James Bible?

Second, why would God sign off with a "talk to you later"? "I will reveal more unto you, hereafter; therefore, let this suffice for the present" (132:66). Could it be that Smith thought he had accomplished his present agenda but knew that this issue wasn't going away and thought he better leave an easy opening to drop another prophecy about plural marriage when the need arises?

Third, why does the LDS Church need to acknowledge in the Introduction to D&C 132 that Smith was personally aware of these principles as early as 1831, even though the prophecy didn't drop until 1843? Could it be that the church is aware of church history and needs some preemptive cover when ordinary Mormons discover the truth, which is that Smith was practicing plural marriage long before he dropped D&C 132 to sanction it?

Fourth, why didn't Emma Smith continue on with the Latter Day Saints after Joseph Smith died? Could it be that she saw her marriage bed defiled (Hebrews 13:4) for many years but was forced into accepting it by a controlling man? Was she torn between wanting to trust that her husband is a prophet and the moral law inside of her (her conscience) that knew that plural marriages were not commanded by God?

Fifth, if this revelation was such progress, such a restoration to God's original intent for the Church, then why has the current LDS Church backed away from the actual practice of it? Why aren't their teenage girls aspiring to be plural wives of the most exalted men in the LDS church?

Sixth, why are people like Warren Jeffs some of the most strident proponents and practitioners of D&C 132? Joseph Smith finished the revelation with "I will reveal more unto you, hereafter; therefore, let this suffice for the present" (132:66), so why didn't he come back with some seat belts to keep men from adding underage wives? Could it be that Smith's wives started as young as 14 years old?

Seventh, why were so many people in Illinois angry with Joseph Smith? Could it be that his teachings were affecting a lot of people who had daughters, granddaughters, nieces, and sisters being brought into unhealthy plural marriages or could potentially be brought in?

Eighth, wasn't it illegal in Illinois to take plural wives? Could it be that Joseph Smith thought he was a law unto himself and had no regard for the Romans 13 imperative to remain subject to the governing authorities, which includes both federal and state laws?

Ninth, doesn't the command to "let mine handmaid, Emma Smith, receive all those that have been given unto my servant Joseph" include two sets of sisters? Could it be that Joseph wasn't very careful when reading Leviticus 18 and put words in God's mouth that contradict the earlier command to never marry two sisters?

Tenth and finally, aren't the deeds of the flesh said to be **evident** in Galatians 5—the first three being sexual in nature? Could it be that there is an evident motive for Joseph Smith to drop D&C 132—the gratification of his flesh with many women?

There are other motivations that become apparent when studying the writings of Joseph Smith. The King Elder Follett discourse betrays a bitter rivalry with Alexander Campbell and other Christian ministers. There is a clear desire for respect, power, and significance in all that he writes. To have ancient prophets foretelling your arrival, to have titles like seer, revelator, prophet, and apostle, to have Priesthood authority, to have keys of the kingdom to bind and loose and forgive, to be followed by the Church of Jesus Christ of Latter Day Saints does wonders for the ego.

We have to compare the evident motives of Joseph Smith to those of Jesus Christ. When Joseph Smith died, he went down shooting. He killed two men and died with a revolver in his hand. Compare him to Jesus. "For even the Son of Man did not come to be served, but to serve, and to give His life a ransom for many" (Mark 10:45). No one can question that Jesus was motivated by selfless love, but the prophecies of Joseph Smith are just too self-serving to be believable.

CONCLUSION

Joseph Smith fails each of the seven Biblical tests of a prophet. That doesn't make Mormons any worse people than anyone else; it makes them deceived. But the wonderful thing about Light is that it makes things visible. When the light shines, it shows forth things for what they are. The wonderful news for Mormons is that having seen the Light, they are free to come into it. There is nothing to fear. The dreaded penalties for apostasy would only hold terror for those who believe that those penalties were prescribed by God. But Joseph Smith's prophecies did not come from God.

First, what Smith wrote was **inconsistent** with God's prior revelation. Malachi 3:6 says that God cannot change, but Smith says He did. Deuteronomy 6:4 says that there is only one God, but Smith says that humans can progress to become gods. Colossians 1:16 says that Jesus created all angels, whether good or fallen, but Smith says that Satan is the spirit-brother of Jesus.

Second, what Smith **predicted** in the name of the Lord did not come to pass. He spoke for God saying that a Temple would be raised up in Independence, Missouri within that generation, but it simply did not happen. Since Deuteronomy 18:20-22 clearly says that one such failure absolutely disqualifies a self-proclaimed prophet, this one failed attempt was devastating. But it was still worse than that. It corresponds to the core of Smith's teaching, which centered around the Temple. Since the prediction failed, we are all the more certain that the theology failed as well.

Third, what Smith produced in terms of the **fruit** of his life was obviously bad. Using only the earliest Mormon sources, it is easy to demonstrate that Smith had a pattern of terrible sexual immorality. He did not genuinely repent of this. Rather, he dropped D&C 132 to justify it and institutionalize it. Furthermore, the current LDS Church has been seeking for years to join the American Christian mainstream, but Smith was the most divisive of all ministers. His ministry was marked by rivalry, envy, bitterness, malice, and every form of contempt for anyone who publicly refuted his theology. What's more, he practiced sorcery. He took the Temple rites from occultic Masonry. He died with a Jupiter Talisman in his pocket. He practiced glass-looking and recited the Book of Mormon with a Seer stone in his hat and his face planted in it.

Fourth, Smith lacked the **miracles** that would be expected from anyone whose authority supersedes both Moses and Jesus. Someone may say that he never claimed that much, but his assertion that his book is the most correct of all books forces that necessary conclusion. In effect—in actual practice—what Joseph Smith "translated" would take a higher place than what was given through Moses and Jesus. But look at the miracles that attended the ministries of Moses and Jesus! God validated them with power. He did not validate Joseph Smith. Even the very people who signed their names as witnesses to Smith's alleged great miracle ended up writing against Smith until their dying day. Smith's own 1832 story about how he saw Jesus in 1820, had by 1840 morphed into a story of a vision of the Father and the Son. None of Smith's claims meet the definition of a miracle. They weren't done in front of the masses, so that no one could deny. They were done in a corner, unlike Moses' and Jesus' public ministries (Acts 26:26).

Fifth, the Book of Mormon establishes subjective experience as the **measure** of truth, but even this testifies against Smith. The experience of Lynn Wilder, Micah Wilder and others can account for the burning in the bosom, but the Mormon experience cannot account for their later testimony of Jesus Christ. Additionally, 99% of the world bears testimony that Smith is not a prophet of God. God is able to give subjective impressions to the human heart and that is why so many Mormons who set out to read the New Testament with the faith of a child will come to the powerful conclusion that the Bible—not the Book of Mormon—is the true Word of God.

Sixth, there are completely disqualifying **accuracy** issues in Joseph Smith's body of work. The fact that he added entire paragraphs to the Book of Isaiah in his translation of the Bible, which were simply not there when the Dead Sea Scrolls were discovered in 1947, is proof positive that Smith was a fraud. He changed the Bible and his sin found him out! He also changed Romans 4:5 to make it say the opposite of what it does. But even canonized texts like the Book of Abraham bear absolutely nothing in common with the actual papyrus from which it was "translated". Mormon apologists can bob and weave on this, but Egyptologists can read Egyptian Hieroglyphics nowadays, and Smith's translation is a fraud. The Book of Mormon is also a fraud since archeology of North America, DNA testing on native Americans, and every other objective test for accuracy proves Smith a liar.

Seventh, Joseph Smith's **motives** are as transparent as Warren Jeffs' motives. D&C 132 justified his own sexual immorality and bullied Emma Smith into putting up with it. His self-aggrandizing Elder King Follett Discourse betrays a hunger for power, significance, and respect. Just test Smith's prophecies by the requirement that 1 Corinthians 13 places upon prophecies. Compare how Smith benefitted himself with the prophecies he dropped with how Jesus benefitted the world. Jesus gave His own flesh for others while Smith served his own flesh.

The Biblical tests have been employed. The reader is now accountable to expose Joseph Smith for who he was. Many Mormons are held in fear. In their hearts they already know that Smith was a false prophet. But they fear that they are wrong, and if they are wrong (this is how cult leaders control their followers), then they are the ones for whom hell was made. How can anyone be sure that Smith wasn't a prophet? He or she simply needs to trust the Bible. The seven tests of a prophet employed in this book came from God's book. God Himself provided Deuteronomy 13 & 18, Matthew 7:15-23, John 14:11, Matthew 7:1-2, John 3:12, and Mark 10:45. These passages expose Joseph Smith as a false prophet, so rejecting Smith is really a matter of trusting God.

God is also the only One who can convince you about the truth of it. It is my prayer that as you think about the words of the Scripture, your heart will be strangely warmed. My prayer for you, friend, is that the Holy Spirit will draw you to faith in Jesus Christ as you hear the words of the Bible.

Jesus is the Son of God. He died on the cross, was buried, and rose from the dead. This He did in order to save you from your sins. He truly loves you. As the greatest friend, He laid down His life in your place. He took the death penalty that you and I deserve. Having risen from the dead, Jesus has opened the way for you and I to have eternal life. God will gladly forgive your sins if you place your trust in His Son alone. Believe in the Lord Jesus Christ and you will be saved.

If you find yourself believing as you read these words, then why not pray right now to invite Jesus Christ—the One described in the Bible, not the counterfeit declared by a false prophet—to take away your sins and become your Lord and Savior? Tell Him that you repent of your sins, including allegiance to a false prophet. Ask for forgiveness. Ask for deliverance, so that you are not controlled by sin anymore. Just call upon Jesus to save you. Pray to receive Him right now.

If you did that, then please find a Bible-believing Church in your area to attend. I am part of a Calvary Chapel, and there is probably one near where you live too. But there are many wonderful churches across America and all around the world. The key is finding a faithful church that has not forsaken the Word of God or denied Christ's Name.

Once you have a true church, you should be baptized. This is a symbolic act, but it is also important. By going under the water and coming up, you identify with Christ's death and resurrection. It is the first step of obedience that you need to take, which will demonstrate that you have new life in Him.

It is also important that you get a Bible and begin reading. Even a little bit each day can make all the difference in your new life, now that you are a Christian (which you are if you genuinely believe in the Jesus of the Bible). Finally, pray all the time. You can do so in the privacy of your own mind or out loud among other believers, but talk to your God and Savior.

If you have not yet placed your faith in Jesus, I pray that you will, and I implore you to do so very soon. We do not know when the Day of the Lord will arrive. We do not know the day of our own death. That is why it is so important to receive the words of Hebrews 4:7, "Today if you hear his voice, do not harden you hearts".

APPENDIX A

RUNNING FROM THE TRUTH

God is greater than our hearts (1 John 3:20), so His truth is more important than our feelings. The Second Letter of John emphasizes truth, mentioning it 5 times in the first 4 verses. John's third epistle says "true" or "truth" 7 times in the 15 verses of the letter. Both of these letters exhort believers to uphold truth in the midst of deception. Likewise Jude initially sat down to write a letter that celebrates salvation, but the Spirit compelled him to change directions and appeal to believers to "contend earnestly for the faith which was once for all handed down to the saints" (Jude 1:3). The truth was under attack. Truth would prevail and be handed down from generation to generation, but not without contention. Children of God who "walk in the truth" (3 John 1:4) must not shrink back from contention, because even though we may not feel good about having to contend, truth is worth fighting for.

God commands Christians to "contend earnestly" (Jude 1:3) and refute those who contradict the truth (Titus 1:9), especially those who contradict truth while claiming to be Christian. We ought to stand for the truth without regard for how we feel. Soldiers don't go to battle only when feeling happy. When threats rise against the truth of God, that is the time to engage.

Those who run from contention because of their own unpleasant feelings act like children. Young children especially are known for making decisions based upon how they are feeling in a given moment. As a child grows up, hopefully he learns to allow truth to take the driver's seat in his life. The mature man still has a place for his feelings, but that place is not behind the wheel. Feelings can come along for the ride, and sometimes offer advice like a backseat driver, but feelings are best kept in the back seat, under the control of truth. If feelings are the parent behind the wheel, the car and everyone in it are in grave danger. Whereas truth always keeps a steady course, feelings are prone to veer off in the wrong direction unexpectedly, without a moment's notice. Great destruction awaits those who never grow up, who take the wheel of their lives with their faces buried in the hat of their own feelings.

Whenever I bring the truth of God's Word to Mormon missionaries, they respond like children. It's ok with me that some of them wear their emotions on their sleeves, but I fear for them when they continually allow their feelings to control their decisions. I go to them with love in my heart. I speak graciously. I listen patiently. I can testify that God keeps my heart at perfect peace. Those who have witnessed these interactions can testify that I never display a contentious attitude. But I do bring the Word of God directly to bear upon the teachings of the LDS Church. I contend earnestly for the doctrines of the Bible and refute those who contradict. Since one of the distinctive qualities of Light is that it forces darkness to flee, it does not surprise me that when the spirit of error is confronted with the truth, it runs and hides. That is exactly what the Mormon missionaries do when I witness to them. But Mormon missionaries have a different explanation for why they run. They cite the same feeling that other liberal Bible teachers experience when confronted with the truth.

Matthew Vines was bold enough to write "God and the Gay Christian". He also found the strength inside himself to make a Youtube video. It is possible to have a semblance of courage and still be childish. When his video went viral, Vines became a theology teacher to hundreds of thousands of people (James 3:1). But he refuses to interact with Dr. Michael Brown who holds different "interpretations" of the Biblical texts that Matthew Vines teaches. Even though Dr. Brown has an impeccable track record of speaking graciously with those with whom he disagrees, Matthew Vines will not defend his interpretations of God's Word. He evidently does not value truth. It hurts his feelings to hear that he is wrong, so he is not able to stand up as a Titus 1 elder to contend for truth. My intent in calling him out is by no means ungracious. I do not mean to single him out, but to point out that running from truth is the consistent response of all liberal approaches to the Bible when confronted with the plain truth of the Bible. If you go forth preaching the Bible, then isn't it your responsibility to defend your doctrine when Bible-believing God-fearing Christians come to examine what you teach? Matthew Vines, like a Mormon missionary, teaches false doctrines and runs from genuine Christians because of the unpleasant feelings he experiences when he is confronted with the truth.

God entrusts elders with safeguarding His doctrine (Titus 1), but some who call themselves "Elder so and so" are not old enough in the faith to carry out an elder's responsibility. One of them answered "no" when I asked him if he had read the entirety of the New Testament! While genuine elders in non-LDS churches often have entire books of the New Testament memorized, many Mormon missionaries have never read the very books that the office of elder is entrusted to defend! They cannot defend their doctrines when we open the Scriptures to them, and that is why they resort to acting like children.

It is unsettling for anyone to hear "you are wrong". But if you are not right, you will not be able to refute those who stand upon the truth of God's Word. Postmodern America rejects these categories of right and wrong altogether. But that is only a symptom of rejecting the truth of God's Word. I love Mormons enough to point out this evident truth. If you are truly walking in the Light as God is in the Light, then you will not experience dark feelings when someone comes to you holding out the words of God's inspired text.

I took the time to write this book because I am an evangelist, not a hater. I want to reach Mormons with the Gospel of God's grace in the same way that I want to reach everyone else. I spend most of my ministry time evangelizing in the inner city. When our team encounters children and adults who have never heard about Christ and Him crucified, we simply share Jesus with them. But we have learned that religious people who already have a view of the Bible need interaction on their terms. When speaking to Muslims, I know that they understand something different than what I mean when I use Gospel terms. In order to reach them, we will have to discuss the differences in our theology and define what we mean by our terminology. The same holds true when I witness to Jehovah's Witnesses, Oneness Pentecostals, Social Gospel Activists, and African Hebrew Israelites. The latter group is only willing to heap abuse upon me, because they consider me a "white devil", so I may not be able to speak with them. But should I just leave all religious people to their own deceptions? To whom would Paul have evangelized if he ignored all the pagans of Rome, leaving them to the gods they already have?

The drug dealers on the corners are more open to hearing the Gospel than are the Mormon missionaries we encounter on the streets of Philadelphia. An occasional drug dealer will threaten to put a bullet in my head, but most listen attentively under what appears to be an almost palpable conviction of sin, which comes from the Holy Spirit. By contrast, one would think that we were carrying guns instead of Bibles when Mormon missionaries see us coming. I don't run from drug dealers, because God keeps my heart at perfect peace when I go out witnessing. Why do Mormon missionaries run from me? It's not as if any of them have been willing to really listen to me for 5 minutes in order to determine whether or not I speak the truth. Rather, their feelings are behind the wheel.

Mormon missionaries have happy feelings when they speak forth their theology, but like a shadow running from the sun, their happiness departs when I quote Scripture to them. They do not feel peace, as I do. They do not feel strength to contend for the truth, as I do. They do not feel concern for my eternal soul, as I have for theirs. They feel only darkness and emptiness. They have described it to me in those terms. Yet, this feeling is what they trust, because this is what they have been taught to trust. The love of God shed abroad in the human heart will "rejoice with the truth" (1 Corinthians 13:6), but the hearts of Mormons are provoked against me if I even ask a question, like "do you believe Romans 4:5 as it is translated in the King James Version of the Bible?" If a person is not willing to listen to the sure testimony of the Lord, which makes wise the simple (Psalm 19:7), then "who can discern his errors" (Psalm 19:12)? Where is the humility and honesty that God requires of those who would desire to receive truth from the Bible (Proverbs 2)? Are Mormons really open to receiving the truth of the Bible?

I must freely admit that before reading the Book of Mormon, I already thought that it was the invention of the highly imaginative and demonically influenced mind of Joseph Smith. When a Mormon missionary gave me one to read, I wasn't really open to believing it. I liked the missionary well enough. What's more, I had a generally favorable opinion of Mormons I knew about—like Mitt Romney, Glenn Beck, Jimmer Fredette, and the writers of Napoleon Dynamite. But I was opposed to the Book of Mormon before I even started to read it because I knew that there were contradictions between LDS theology and the Bible, which I had already received as unadulterated truth.

I was already convinced that the Book of Mormon did not come from God when I read it. I was not in a receptive posture because I was satisfied in my relationship with the Lord Jesus Christ. I had a deep and profound sense that there was nothing missing or broken there. I had heard enough about the life and doctrine of Joseph Smith to convince me that he had no precious thing to offer. I believed what the Bible plainly said. What more could I need? The burden of proof was not upon a Bible-believing Christian but upon the Book of Mormon, which testified of itself that it was Another Testament of Jesus Christ, comparable to the Bible.

I admit that I lacked faith in the Book of Mormon when I first picked it up. I admit this because even as I picked up the Book of Mormon feeling that I had nothing to gain from it, those raised in Mormon homes and Mormon subcultures often pick it up with the hope of gaining their testimony. They bring preconceived ideas and motivations to the text just as much (or more) than I did. They feel that if they never gain a testimony to the truth of the book, they have everything to lose. It is not uncommon to hear about lost, strained or broken family relationships, lost friendships, lost opportunities, lost loves, and other losses when young Mormons grow up and lose their religion. Growing up Mormon makes it hard to read the Book of Mormon without the influence of already wanting to believe it, in the same way that being a committed Christian makes it hard to read the Book of Mormon without rejecting it before the text has a chance to speak for itself.

The difference is that Christians were commanded to "hold fast the faithful word" (Titus 1:9) of the Bible long before the Book of Mormon was written, so presupposing error in the latter rather than the former when the texts disagree is an outworking of obedient wisdom. Those who have any measure of faith in the Book of Mormon prior to testing it against the Word of God are unwisely allowing their own feelings and preconceived ideas to drive their perception.

The key to escaping Mormonism is recognizing the error of the standard for determining Truth that the Introduction of the Book of Mormon commends to the reader. It doesn't say to check the content of the Book of Mormon against the earlier revelations found in the Bible, like a good Berean would (Acts 17:11). Rather, the reader is essentially instructed to read, pray, and trust that the Holy Spirit will confirm the message. At first glance, this test almost sounds acceptable. But no parameters were given for what constitutes Holy Spirit confirmation, so in the end, the reader is really being told to trust his own judgment of what feels right. Certainly, the Holy Spirit is able to affect human emotions. He affects mine all the time. But Muslims claim to have profound feelings when reading the Qur'an. Secular humanists feel strong passions when pursuing their agendas. Buddhists reach Nirvana. No matter the religion, the human heart is dangerously capable of producing emotional epiphanies that a religion is true.

Was the author of the Introduction to the Book of Mormon aware that Satan is able to produce counterfeit experiences (2 Corinthians 11)? If so, then why appeal to subjective experience as the ultimate measure of truth? Isn't there a higher authority than the impressions of the human heart? What about the seven objective tests of a prophet that we find in the Bible? Does the reader know where to find these tests in the Bible? "What Every Mormon Needs to See" tells the reader to employ these Biblical tests rather than relying primarily upon private impressions in the sometimes-deceitful human heart.

I was surprised by the threats I read in the Book of Mormon. The Mormon missionary used an analogy with me that taught about how we all need to focus more upon our similarities and less upon our differences. He said that when a few coins are set before someone and the person is asked to describe them, the test subject will almost always describe the coins according to what makes them different, rather than what makes them similar. The point of the missionary's analogy was to say that it is a sad fact of human nature that we fail to focus on similarities. According to the missionary, mainstream Christians need to look at Mormons as Christians who share a common faith in Jesus Christ despite the minor differences. But that is not at all the tone of the Book of Mormon.

The Book of Mormon remained consistent with Joseph Smith's view of others who are called by the Name of Christ. In Joseph's 1832 version of the first vision, Joseph had already arrived at a conclusion by studying the Scriptures. In the 1838 version of the story, the Father and the Son (it was only one personage in the 1832 version) tell him something that had "never entered [his] heart". Regardless of how he came to this conclusion, it is clear that Joseph thought that "all [the churches] were wrong". The Book of Mormon doesn't walk back Joseph's epiphany by saying that the errors are only minor doctrinal differences between genuine Christians. Rather, the Book of Mormon raises the stakes by claiming that if someone doesn't accept the validity and distinct theology of the Book of Mormon, he is under a curse.

The prophet Mormon says that the Book of Mormon "is written for the intent that ye may believe [the Bible]; and if ye believe that ye will believe this also" (Mormon 7:9). But this doesn't mean that the reader is free to take or leave the Book of Mormon. Speaking of the revelations about the Jaredites, Moroni says of him "that shall deny these things, let him be accursed" (Ether 4:8). 3 Nephi 29:4 echoes this sentiment. It warns the reader that "the sword of his justice is in the right hand" to bring a curse upon those who reject God's latter-day revelations. When I read the Book of Mormon, it seemed to me that the prophets in the text struck the same divisive chord as did Joseph Smith, quite different from the more conciliatory tone of today's missionaries.

When I read the Book of Mormon, I was most alarmed by what I didn't read. I was disturbed by the near absence of distinct LDS theology. The gradualism of LDS proselytizing is very dangerous. A potential convert is not given the King Follett Discourse, the Book of Abraham, or even Doctrine and Covenants when they first meet with LDS missionaries. Rather, he is given a Book of Mormon. As the person reads it, he will be struck by how closely the theology seems to relate to that of the Bible. Those who are not well rooted (Colossians 2:6-8) in the Bible will not catch the different view of universal atonement unto resurrection (2 Nephi 9:15). They will hear the rampant usage of Biblical phrases, but they may not catch the twisting of Ephesians 2:8-9 to say "it is by grace that we are saved, after all we can do" (2 Nephi 25:23).

Those unfamiliar with LDS theology may sympathize with the prophet Moroni begging the reader to overlook his imperfections (Mormon 8:12). They may conclude that this poor little prophet is innocuous. Why not overlook little contradictions and occasional absurdities? The barges in Ether 2:24 could just be a miracle. Who has "reformed Egyptian" (Mormon 9:32) to study it? It is endearing when the prophet catches himself (9:30) and excuses himself (9:31). The author of the Book of Mormon comes across as just another Christian who only wants someone to love him and accept him. His oddities are what make him special. But there's no danger here. Or is there danger here? There is danger when Satan disguises himself as an angel of light (2 Corinthians 11).

The Trinitarianism of Joseph Smith in 1929 is the most deceptive aspect of the Book of Mormon. Rather than Elohim and Jehovah being different beings and different gods in later LDS theology, in 2 Nephi 19:6, Jesus is Everlasting Father. Joseph Smith mistakenly calls the Holy Spirit "it" (2 Nephi 32:5), instead of "He" (John 14-16) as the Bible does. When Jesus can no longer hide "the body of my spirit" (Ether 3:16, 12:20), there is a hint that Joseph has some strange thoughts. So, Joseph Smith's Trinitarianism is clearly weak, but there is no doubt that the Book of Mormon attempts to affirm the Trinity! The prophet Amulek tells Zeezrom that there is not more than one God (Alma 11:28-29). There is no hint that men will progress to become gods of other worlds. In fact, King Benjamin affirms the orthodox Christian view of the afterlife. "My immortal spirit may join the choirs above in singing the praises of a just God" (Mosiah 2:28).

The Book of Mormon says nothing about Jesus and Satan being Spirit brothers. It says nothing about us in a preexistent spirit form sustaining Jesus to be our Savior in this world. It says nothing about Elohim being a part of a counsel of the Gods. It says nothing about Elohim having a spirit wife. It doesn't even tell us about the telestial, terrestrial, and celestial levels of heaven. It says nothing about the work one must do in the Temple in order to attain to the celestial and have a chance to progress to become a God. It certainly doesn't say what Brigham Young later said about Joseph standing guard to approve those who would enter in (Journal of Discourses, Vol. 7, pp 282-291).

The reader of the Book of Mormon is in grave danger because he is not being told the real story! He is only told a fun tale about Native Americans. But if he buys the tale, then he also comes away with one crucial thing. He believes in the modern-day seer. He accepts the authority of Joseph Smith. It will only take a few years for gradualism to run its course. The proselyte will accept the later revelations of the modern-day prophet if his subjective testimony was a strong enough experience in his life. Mormon missionaries run like the wind when they hear these truths plainly stated. But if I have spoken contrary to the Bible, then it is their responsibility to show me where. They run because they know that they cannot stand up to what the Bible plainly says. If you are a Mormon or have been flirting with becoming one, the Bible calls you to run—don't walk—to the Jesus of whom it testifies.

APPENDIX B

REVIEW OF THE BOOK OF MORMON

What is the integrating theme that explains the phenomenon that is the Book of Mormon? Is there an adequate theory that integrates all the internal evidence in the book, that takes into account the external evidence about the life of the author, and that offers an explanation for what the book is? There certainly are spiritual forces behind the book, and since the book contradicts the Bible, those spirits are certainly evil. Demons inspired the author, but from a human level, the integrating theme of the Book of Mormon is the attempt of an aspiring prophet to validate himself through the writings of former prophets. I discerned this theme in the Book of Mormon because of a previous study that Jochen Katz, a researcher from answering-islam.com, made of the Qur'an and its author.

Joseph actually employed the same old tactic that was used at least once before by an aspiring prophet seeking validation from others. In the same way that the Qur'an is the validation of Muhammad's theology and prophetic status placed into the mouths of *former prophets*, the Book of Mormon etches Joseph's theology and prophetic status upon plates of metal engraved by the hands of *former prophets*. Real prophets of old gave genuine testimony of Jesus Christ, but imaginary friends testified of Muhammad and Joseph. The former prophets that the Qur'an and the Book of Mormon talk about are like alter egos of Muhammad and Joseph. The lives of the former prophets embodied everything that their creator hoped to become. Like the false prophet in the Book of

Revelation (13:11-18), they affirm everything their Beast believes. They preach their master's theology. They tell of his life. They curse those who would dare identify the Beast for who he is. They do the dirty work that allows the man himself to preach "peace, peace", when there is no peace.

Muhammad's Qur'an has Jesus prophetically affirming Salat and Zakat (2 of the 5 Pillars of Islam) from the cradle. Never mind that the earliest textual evidence for Jesus' words in Surah 19 is the appearance of the Qur'an itself in the 600s AD. Putting the words in the mouth of Jesus apparently adds weight. In the same way, Adam, Noah, Abraham, Moses, and David all appear in the Qur'an. They all act like Muhammad. They all preach his theology. They herald his coming (Surah 7:157). As you begin to study them, it becomes obvious that the new version of the characters includes changes from the Old Testament version in a way that benefits Muhammad's situation. It seems to escape faithful Muslims that the earliest textual evidence for their prophetic record is the appearance of the Qur'an itself. What value does a prophetic record have if it only predicts things that have already happened at the time the prophecy is recorded?

The Book of Isaiah is a valuable record of predictive prophecy because it can be clearly shown that it was written long before the time of Christ, and yet it clearly speaks of Him. The Great Isaiah Scroll from the Dead Sea Scrolls is protected under thick glass, and rightly so, because ancient manuscripts like that are valuable. Whatever the free market says they are worth, Christians should recognize the inestimable value of history written in advance. All 39 books of the Hebrew Bible have been proven to have been written long before the time of Jesus Christ, and yet each one clearly speaks of Him. In my book "Faith Before Sight", I demonstrate how every Old Testament book is a validation of Jesus Christ, because each one speaks of Him long in advance of His coming.

Everything in the Book of Mormon validates Joseph Smith's ministry and theology, yet there isn't a shred of evidence that it was written ahead of time. We have no plates to study, but as a first-time reader of the Book of Mormon, I couldn't help but notice that every prophet from Lehi to Moroni couldn't stop talking about "the plates"! For me, it begged the question of why. Would it help Joseph Smith, would it somehow validate him, if earlier prophets were preoccupied with the plates? Of course it would. If other prophets before Joseph were busy burying and digging up plates, if Gadianton robbers buried their treasures, only to have them become slippery in the earth (Mormon 1:18), then the man charged in 1826 for glass-looking is not a wild-eyed treasure hunter. He is a seer, completely consistent with the prophets of old. Never mind that no prophet in the Old Testament ever made or buried plates. Ever since the writing of the Book of Mormon, Joseph is not alone.

Joseph is also not the first prophet to bring forth Scripture or see God's instructions using "seer stones". Sensible Christians in 19th Century America may consider it sorcery to bury one's face in a hat and, by the use of seer stones, call back voices from the dust. But if so godly a man as Nephi (2 Nephi 5:12) used the stones as well, then this must be what prophets do. Such is the power of a story on the human emotion. Never mind that the Urim and Thummim were particular stones affixed in a certain way to the High Priest's vesture (Leviticus 8:8), and the High Priest himself was required to descend from Levi in order to be one (Deuteronomy 18:1). If there were other priests with different stones and a new set of rules (that contradict the former), then on the basis of their example, Joseph is not a sorcerer.

The Book of Mormon even contains direct prophecies about Joseph Smith, and how strongly would Joseph be validated if 2 Nephi 27 was nothing but a quotation from Isaiah 29! Then the Great Isaiah Scroll would include these parts about Joseph, his three witnesses, and his other friends and family who were willing to sign Joseph's documents. When Martin Harris admitted in 1838 that they had only seen the plates with spiritual eyes, many left the LDS Church. Unlike Jesus' Apostles who gladly gave their lives for Him, except for Joseph's family, every one of Joseph's witnesses played the Judas to him. Joseph wouldn't have known these eventualities when he wrote about his witnesses in 2 Nephi 27. The Book was published in 1830, before they left the church. But what genuine validation it would have been if the following words actually appeared in Isaiah, and would have thus been written ahead of time.

Wherefore, at that day when the book shall be delivered unto the man of whom I have spoken, the book shall be hid from the eyes of the world, that the eyes of none shall behold it save it be that three witnesses shall behold it, by the power of God, besides him to whom the book shall be delivered; and they shall testify to the truth of the book and the things therein. And there is none other which shall view it, save it be a few according to the will of God, to bear testimony of his word unto the children of men; for the Lord has said that the words of the faithful should speak as if it were from the dead. Wherefore, the Lord God will proceed to bring forth the words of the book; and in the mouth of as many witnesses as seemeth him good will he establish his word; and wo be unto him that rejecteth the word of God! (2 Nephi 27: 12-14)

If these words appeared at any point before Joseph's day, they would be remarkable! But as it stands, they strongly validate Joseph Smith only in the way that Muhammad's Qur'an strongly validates him. They lack one essential ingredient to the making of predictive prophecy—evidence that the words were written long before the events they describe. Where is the Great Nephi Scroll that would turn 2 Nephi 27:12-14 into predictive prophecy? But no one should miss that the purpose of these words is nothing other than the validation of Joseph Smith through the etchings of a former prophet named Nephi.

If indeed there have been plain and precious parts of the Bible gone missing, isn't it ironic that these are they that testify of Joseph? John 5:29 is turned on its head. It is just too rich to swallow. LDS Scripture (Pearl of Great Price, Articles of Faith, Article 8) affirms a belief in the Bible "as far as it is translated correctly". The Book of Mormon says that plain and precious teachings have gone missing (1 Nephi 13:40). In 2 Nephi, the Book of Mormon literally quotes 14 entire chapters of the King James Version of the Book of Isaiah. Only the last chapter quoted (Isaiah 29) restores any plain and precious thing to the allegedly corrupted text of Isaiah. The one thing that 2 Nephi 27 adds to the King James Version of Isaiah 29, the only thing the Book of Mormon restores to Isaiah, is the part that testifies of Joseph!

The missing part of Isaiah just so happened to be about the way the Book of Mormon shall be delivered and about those who will witness its recovery. When the Book of Mormon gives us the chance to look at 14 chapters of Isaiah after being purified from translation error, after restoring the missing plain and precious teachings, what beautiful new revelations do we find? It turns out that nothing went missing or got mistranslated except for that which validates Joseph. If there was only one thing that God should have protected in the textual tradition of Isaiah 29, it should have been the part that validates the restorer! Since Joseph is going to give us an authority that supersedes the texts we have of the Bible (uncorrupted Scripture trumps corrupted), then wouldn't God be willing to let every last word of Isaiah go missing before letting the part about Joseph disappear? After all, the Book of Mormon is able to bring back the words of Isaiah from the dust. But lo and behold, the only part that God allowed to go missing was the part about Joseph.

Even without this all-too-convenient restoration, think logically for a moment about the implications of having 13 chapters of the Book of Mormon come forth by dictation without reference to the KJV and turn out to be exactly the same. If God only protected the corruptible text insofar as it says nothing of a restoration, then what was the point of protecting anything at all? But answer that however one may, more than 13 chapters of 2 Nephi confirm that our textual tradition as translated into the King James Version of the Bible is without even a single misspelled word! If we cannot assume from the verbatim similitude of 13 chapters of the Book of Mormon and the KJV that God supernaturally protects His Word from even the slightest error, then we must conclude that Joseph simply read the corruptible KJV as he dictated the Book of Mormon. But it is logically absurd to say that 13 chapters supernaturally appeared in Joseph's hat without the slightest variation from what the KJV published in 1611 without also affirming that God supernaturally kept the 1611 KJV from error. Joseph cannot have it both ways. He cannot give us the very words of the KJV, narrowly escape the charge of plagiarism by asserting supernatural reception of his book, and then turn around and say that the KJV was not supernaturally protected.

You cannot have 13 verbatim chapters (thousands of words—all identical) without saying that both sides of the match are supernaturally incorruptible! Nothing has to be supernatural if you admit that one side copied from the other. But the 1830 side of the match will not admit to making use of the 1611 side. So, logic requires the Book of Mormon to admit that for God to bring the KJV forth in 1611 without deviancy (nothing missing, nothing added, not even one minor textual deviant after more than 2,300 years from when Isaiah wrote those 13 chapters) would require a miracle as large as the bringing forth of the Book of Mormon.

Without one copying the other, the identical words found in the 13 chapters of KJV Isaiah and 2 Nephi requires a statistical impossibility—a miracle—on *both* sides of the match. The actual English words match *exactly*. Yet the Book of Mormon wants to have its cake and eat it too. It wants a perfect analogue with 13 chapters of KJV Isaiah. That would require that God perfectly protected KJV Isaiah from corruption. Then it wants to turn around and devour KJV Isaiah by alleging that a few verses of Isaiah 29 slipped through the clumsy fingers of scribes somewhere along the bumpy road of history. Hasn't it considered what Divine intervention would have been necessary to render exactly the right words for 13 chapters after it had been 2,300 years since the original words were written (in an altogether-different language)? Why then did the Divine One suddenly stop working and let just a few verses arbitrarily drop from His 1611 translation? This absurdity becomes dangerous when the only missing piece turns out to be that which establishes Joseph as the only real authority going forward.

The Book of Mormon, like the Qur'an, is validation for a modern-day prophet written back into the mouths of former prophets. 2 Nephi 27:12-14 directly prophesies of Joseph in order to make him a direct fulfillment of a prophecy. Since this portion of writing is nowhere to be found in any textual evidence prior to 1830, it is clear what it is. It is a late intrusion upon the text of Isaiah, placed into the mouth of Isaiah by the mouth of the very man who wanted to be a modern day Isaiah. But there are hundreds of other examples in the lives of the imagined prophets of the Book of Mormon where it is evident that Joseph was seeking to establish a precedent for himself.

The appearance of the first family in the Book of Mormon sure would make things better for Joseph as he stood in his family in 1829. Lehi is honored, but isn't really the hero. Like Joseph Smith Sr., Lehi appears mostly as a figurehead and needs to pass the baton as his strength begins to fail him, even though he shouldn't be too old to be the outspoken leader. Nephi is like Joseph Smith Jr.—the real hero of the story. Nephi has an ever-faithful brother named Sam. Always willing to submit to his brother's leadership, he is not unlike Joseph's brother Samuel, save the shortened version of his name. He deserved special recognition for his wholehearted devotion. But William, Don Carlos, and Hiram needed a little more prodding.

Wherefore, it came to pass that I, Nephi, did take my family, and also Zoram and his family, and Sam, mine elder brother and his family, and Jacob and Joseph, my younger brethren, and also my sisters, and all those who would go with me. And all those who would go with me were those who believed in the warnings and the revelations of God; wherefore, they did harken unto my words. (2 Nephi 5:6)

Joseph Smith Jr. strongly desired for his brothers to follow his lead, so he gave them two strong examples of brothers who failed to follow the lead of a former prophet. Laman and Lemuel failed to follow Nephi. Their legacy was a rather strong deterrent if any of Joseph's brothers ever contemplated rejecting Joseph Smith Jr.'s leadership. Joseph Smith Sr. accepted it early on, but his brothers were a tougher sell. After reading the Book of Mormon, none of them dared reject their brother's prophetic status. William and Don Carlos kept a healthy distance, but the example they saw in Nephi's story made it clear how they would be regarded if they outright rejected their brother's claim to be a prophet.

Joseph Smith Jr. wasn't only interested in getting his family on board with him, he wanted as many followers as would join him. Just as Muhammad wrote one of his companions into the story of Noah, Joseph created Zoram to honor men like the Whitmers, Cowdery, and Harris. The characters in Nephi's story certainly set a precedent for Joseph's family and friends. The reader of the Book of Mormon had archetypes to follow, which helped Joseph establish his authority in his fledgling church.

After the first family passed from the text, hundreds of years of history slipped quickly into the forgotten past. The Books of Jacob, Enos, Jarom, Omni, and Mormon attempt a few contributions to the historical record of these hundreds of years, but they seem bent on emphasizing one preeminent concern: the plates. It is striking how much attention is given to plates that preserve history, which plates we do not have!

Could it be that the real function of the plates was to validate Joseph? By making former prophets have plates and care deeply for them, Joseph's story is not unprecedented. Joseph's claim to have received his plates was certainly unique. But being unique in a claim of this kind is not necessarily a benefit. If Joseph was the only prophet in history to be preoccupied with plates, then perhaps someone will chalk it up to the cultural conditioning of a man who spent his teen years searching for treasures in the hills that the Mound Builders left behind in New York. But if prophets of old have always been concerned with preserving plates, then perhaps Joseph was not just a product of his time and place.

The stories in the Book of Mormon certainly help to push the reader toward the conclusion that Joseph's concerns are consistent with those of the former prophets. The Book of Mormon ends with the last of the Nephites clinging to dear life and holding the plates more dearly than life itself. He buries the plates in the ground to be kept until that great day when a prophet like those of old will appear and restore everything to how it used to be. If any record of these prophets could be shown to predate 1830, then perhaps the prophets could speak from the dust and validate Joseph. But as it stands, it appears that Joseph created them to validate himself.

Perhaps the most telling proof for my theory is that the former prophets in the Book of Mormon weigh in on every major theological dispute prevalent in 19th Century America. Joseph the 19th century American preacher suddenly received quite a leg up on the competition when the words of the former prophets finally became unearthed and validated everything that Joseph had been trying to say. Now maybe the world will listen.

Is the majority-view cessationism or the minority-view continuationism correct? Jonathan Edwards opened the door to continuationism in the 1st Great Awakening. During the 2nd Great Awakening, Quakers, Methodists and many other groups were reporting a variety of charismatic experiences. Debates on the subject were raging across America. But the majority view was still decidedly cessationist. Joseph Smith's prophets weighed in with a definitive word from the past. The gifts of the Spirit have not ceased, but continue on to this day. The Book of Mormon weighs in heavily on this theological dispute and hails its triumph over the majority view. But this triumphalism only marks the Book of Mormon as a product of its time relative to what comes later. To the 21st Century reader who lives when a majority of Christians around the world believe in the modern-day operation of spiritual gifts, there is nothing exciting about the Book of Mormon taking that view. It was only bucking the system of the majority 200 years ago. Now it just sounds dated.

It also sounds incredible that continuationist doctrines would be on the mind of prophets who allegedly appeared before the time of Christ. One would think that actual churches and baptizers like Alma would have to appear and make Christians only after the time of Christ. One would think that the gifts of the Spirit listed in 1 Corinthians 12 wouldn't be discussed until at least after Pentecost 33 AD. But 2 Nephi 32:2 evidently anticipated the debate and got out in front of it, 570 years before Christ was even born!

In a similar way, the prophets step in and settle the great debate between Calvinists and Arminians. A view similar to Wesley's prevenient grace is the winner (2 Nephi 9:15). But it more closely resembles the heretical view of the Pelagian heresy (Alma 13:3). Calvinism receives a strong rebuke (Alma 31:16). The language of Alma 31 couldn't be more directed. It is clearly about the great post-reformation divide in Protestantism. Alma weighs in by tying the doctrine of election with flagrant unbelief in Christ (Alma 31:17). He derides double predestination, the idea of being elect unto wrath (31:17). He mocks the word "chosen" (31:18) even though Peter, Paul, and John would probably like to have a word with him about that. Joseph Smith obviously thought that the Calvinists of his day were prideful (31:25), rich, materialistic (31:28) Sunday-morning pretenders (31:23). High church (like that of Episcopalians) and cultural Christianity, where people only talk about God on Sundays, also receives rebuke by caricature (the Zoramites of Alma 31).

The prophets were on board with the Stone-Campbell restorationist movement. Baptism by immersion is necessary for salvation and churches need to be called purely by the name of Christ (Mosiah 18:4, 17). It matters what authority the baptizer has (Mosiah 18:18), but the Alexander Campbell's of the world better not deny that Joseph received revelation (Jacob 7:5).

Joseph Smith's soteriology, and the soteriology of the restorationists that preached just before Joseph (Alexander Campbell and company), was spelled out in detail 600 years before Jesus died for the sins of the world! 2 Nephi 31 lays out Joseph's plan of salvation, as far he had developed it in 1829. The steps are submission to Lordship, baptismal regeneration, charismatic signs, and perseverance of the saints. These theological issues were hotly debated in 19th century America, and Joseph's prophets give a definitive word.

Following the anti-Masonic fervor of 1826 stirred up by the book that Captain William Morgan released in New York, it is not surprising that the Gadianton robbers are introduced in the Book of Mormon to rebuke the secret combinations of the Free Masons. Since all that calmed down later, it is not surprising that Joseph Smith went ahead and became a Free Mason in 1842.

The prevailing view about African descent from Cain and the inferior intelligence of blacks and Native Americans is affirmed (2 Nephi 5:21). Mosiah 27 espouses a healthy view of religious liberty, one of which the founding fathers of the United States would be most proud!

Joseph wants to be a prophet, and more than a prophet—a seer (Mosiah 8:15). He cannot baptize himself into such an office, but if a prophet like Alma baptized himself (Mosiah 18:14), if Abinadi knew about types and shadows (Mosiah 13:10), if a King Benjamin once had a seer gift to interpret plates (Mosiah 21:28), then what keeps Joseph from being a seer? By virtue of the publication of the Book of Mormon in 1830, there is precedent for Joseph to receive the records (Mosiah 22:24) and confer authority (Mosiah 23:17) upon himself. Mosiah not only authorized Alma, he simultaneously authorized Joseph to organize the Church of God (Mosiah 25). The New Testament Church is run by elders, not by priests. But Alma authorizes Joseph's new ecclesiology (Mosiah 25:21). Thus Joseph's seat in America replaces the Pope's seat in Rome, and a new Catholicism is born (Mosiah 26).

It is clear that the prophets of Joseph's Book of Mormon walk in lock step with Joseph's theology, philosophy, and view of reality. The problem is that they give loud voice to everything that mattered in 1829, even when it doesn't make any sense for such early prophets to know about the issues of 19th century America. The writers of the Old and New Testaments certainly didn't speak so directly to the interpretive questions of 19th Century America. What they said was adequate. It was what God truly wanted us to have. But the Book of Mormon makes them look quite deficient.

The Biblical prophets are especially deficient compared to Nephi, King Benjamin, Alma, Jacob and the other new world prophets that went before Christ (BC). David may have his Psalm 22, Isaiah his 4th Servant Song, but Joseph makes his prophets talk about the Messiah as if Nephi were Matthew, Mark, Luke, or John. Before Jesus was born, Joseph Smith's prophets knew as much as the eyewitnesses would! Lehi knows John the Baptist's actual sermons in the actual translated English of the King James Version (1 Nephi 10:8). Joseph's prophets not only know Jesus' name, they know Mary and Joseph's names as well.

They know as much as the inspired Apostles who wrote under the New Covenant, but they don't seem to know much about the Old Covenant. This makes sense if young Joseph Smith read the New Testament a lot, but only skimmed books like Leviticus. When Joseph tries to add something new, he comes up with a miracle whereby Israelites are able to eat uncooked meat without getting sick (1 Nephi 17:12). Had Joseph been adequately familiar with Leviticus, he would not have made Israelites eat meat with blood in it, especially not by

God's decree! Leviticus 17:11-14 is rooted in Genesis 9:4 and is the reason why Israelites would always carefully cook all blood out of their meat before eating it. These are the kinds of things that Old Covenant prophets should have been concerned about. By such laws, God was preparing His people to treasure the blood of Jesus. But Joseph's Old Covenant prophets all but forgot to put blood upon the altar. While the Levites were ministering daily, cleansing nearly everything with blood in the Temple in Jerusalem and offering burnt offerings, peace offerings, sin offerings, and guilt offerings, prophets in America were running around with plates and talking about things that concern the New Covenant, all the while violating the Old Covenant left and right.

All the prophets of the Book of Mormon validate Joseph Smith, but there is no evidence that any of them existed. Joseph had an obvious motive for the crime of imagining them and selling their existence to those who would believe him. If someone believes that Nephi was real, then what he wrote in 2 Nephi 27 is about Joseph Smith, and Joseph is a prophet. But the sad thing is that most Mormons today think that Nephi's prophecy is a quote from Isaiah. Nothing could be further from the truth! One would have to add Nephi's words to the text of Isaiah in order to have them there. Astonishingly, Joseph Smith was even willing to do this. He made his own translation of the Bible, and lo and behold, several paragraphs of new material appear in Isaiah 29, material that validates Joseph as a modern-day restorer. Such is the story of the Book of Mormon.

APPENDIX C

WHO IS OF THE ORDER OF MELCHIZEDEK?

An Excerpt from *Faith Before Sight*

The Scriptures teach that Jesus is the Great and Final High Priest (Hebrews 7:28). A priest is a go-between—an intermediary—one who stands in the gap between a Holy God and sinful people. The primary problem that humanity faces is that we are sinners against a Holy God. We are separated from God on account of our sin. So, we need a Priest who can truly bridge that gap for us. We need Someone who can offer the sacrifice that God requires and deliver the blessing that He gives.

Jesus is that Priest. His descent from Judah makes this hard to believe at first glance. Jacob had 12 sons. The difficulty is that while Judah was chosen to establish the line of the coming *King* (Genesis 49:10), Levi was chosen to establish a line of *priests* (Leviticus 1:7). How could Jesus be the final and Great High Priest if He doesn't descend from Levi? The answer is that while Isaac, Jacob and Levi were still only the coming seed of Abraham (before the descendants of Abraham were conceived), a different Priest appeared on the scene (Genesis 14:18-20). This Priest could have been an ordinary man who was sent to prefigure the coming Christ. More likely, He was Christ Jesus Himself appearing to Abraham and remaining forever in the text of Genesis in order to help us believe in Him when He comes in the flesh to serve as our High Priest.

The Priesthood of which He was a part was a higher order than the one that would proceed from Abraham. We can know that this alternate Priesthood is superior to that which comes through Abraham because the lesser brings an offering to the greater, while the greater blesses the lesser. In the Genesis account, Abraham—the lesser—gives an offering to this Priest. The Priest—the greater—gives a blessing to Abraham.

And Melchizedek king of Salem brought out bread and wine; now he was a priest of God Most High. He blessed him and said, "Blessed be Abram of God Most High, Possessor of heaven and earth; and blessed be God Most High, who has delivered your enemies into your hand." He gave him a tenth of all (Genesis 14:18-20).

The mysterious Priest of Genesis 14 is superior to all the priests who descended from Abraham. This Superior Priest received a tenth of Abraham's possessions and delivered a blessing that only God could fulfill. He bridged the gap between Abraham and God. In so doing, he points us to Jesus Christ in **nine** astonishing ways.

First, the mysterious Priest's name—Melchizedek—means "Righteous King". Is that an appropriate title for Jesus? Jesus has the pedigree of a King because of his descent through Judah (Genesis 49:10) and David (2 Samuel 7:16). As far as His righteousness is concerned, no one has ever shown even one instance where Jesus failed to be righteous. In fact, the Christian claim that Jesus was sinless would need to be true if indeed He was to serve as a Priest that could bring sinful people to a Holy God. Jesus had to have *righteousness* in order to give righteousness away to unrighteous people (Romans 4:5).

"But now apart from the Law the righteousness of God has been manifested, being witnessed by the Law and the Prophets" (Romans 3:21). What is this righteousness that the Law (the Jewish Torah) speaks about, but that doesn't come through obeying the Law? It is the righteousness of the King spoken about in Genesis 14:18. It is what God gave to Abraham in Genesis 15:6 when he "believed God" right after encountering Melchizedek. The "Righteous King" is able to impute His righteousness to others. Because we are sinners, we cannot be righteous unless we are given *righteousness*, "even the righteousness of God through faith in Jesus Christ for all those who believe" (Romans 3:22a). We need a Righteous King to give us the righteousness we couldn't get on our own. We can't keep the Law perfectly, so we need the Righteous King that the Torah speaks about in Genesis 14:18 and 15:6.

Second, this King Melchizedek hailed from Salem, a city whose name literally means "Peace". Jerusalem—the Peace of Jeru—was the City where Jesus served. Taken outside of her gates, He made the ultimate sacrifice and made *peace* between God and humanity.

Therefore, having been justified by faith, we have peace with God through our Lord Jesus Christ (Romans 5:1).

Third, and this stands out strikingly because the words of the mysterious prophecy are so few, Melchizedek "brought out bread and wine" (Genesis 14:18). Anyone who has ever taken "Communion" will recognize the significance of what this Priest brings. On the night Jesus was betrayed, He took *bread* and broke it, saying, "this is my body, which is given for you" (1 Corinthians 11:24). He brought out *wine* and passed the cup, saying, "this is my blood of the covenant, which is poured out for many for the forgiveness of sins" (Matthew 26:28). Jesus the Priest brought the bread and wine of His own flesh and blood.

Fourth, the King and the Priest are one-in-the-same person. The Essenes—a Jewish sect who lived around the caves of Qumran in Israel before and during the time of Jesus—were expecting three Messiahs when Jesus appeared. They looked for one Prophet, one Priest, and one King, because the Scriptures pictured the Anointed One in each of these roles. Until Jesus came, the Kings of Israel were never allowed to serve as Priests. Saul, the first King, was reprimanded for trying to do so (1 Samuel 13). But the earlier appearance of Melchizedek in Genesis 14 included the revelation of the singular greatness of the coming King. Jesus is not only that Lion from the tribe of Judah (Israel's King), but also a Priest, and so much more. He is the embodiment of all that we need.

Fifth, as noted earlier, Melchizedek is greater than Abraham. The greater blesses the lesser. This being so, we naturally want to know more about this great king. Who is this Righteous King-Priest? The entire Jewish system of religion traces its root back to Abraham (as does Islam), but Melchizedek is greater. Jesus is as much greater than Abraham as the builder of a house is greater than the house he builds.

"Surely you are not greater than our father Abraham, who died? The prophets died too; whom do you make yourself out to be?" Jesus answered, "If I glorify myself, My glory is nothing; it is My Father who glorifies Me, of whom you say, 'He is our God'; and you have not come to know Him, but I know Him; and if I say that I do not

know Him, I will be a liar like you, but I do know Him and keep His word. Your father Abraham rejoiced to see My day, and he saw it and was glad." So the Jews said to Him, "You are not yet fifty years old, and have you seen Abraham?" Jesus said to them, "Truly, truly, I say to you, before Abraham was born, I am." (John 8:53-58)

Sixth, that Melchizedek is greater than Abraham is confirmed by the fact that Abraham pays a tithe to Him. "He gave him a tenth of all" (Genesis 14:20). Not only so, Hebrews 7:8 points out that in contrast to mere mortal men who receive tithes on God's behalf—namely, the Levites who were later to appear—Melchizedek is no mere mortal. He received Abraham's tithe as if he were the One to whom tithes are ultimately due. When Christians tithe, they are ultimately giving to God (not to their church, to charity, or to any mortal men). Jesus receives tithes, offerings, and even worship as One to whom it is actually due.

"When they saw [Jesus], they worshipped Him" (Matthew 28:17)

Seventh, this Priest enters the Genesis narrative and exists as if he were from another world. He bursts onto the scene and then disappears, occupying but a couple of sentences in the text. No mention is made of Melchizedek's origin. Nothing is said about where He will go. Yet he accomplishes all of what has been said so far. Jesus, not of this world, but having come from eternity past at the right hand of His Father in heaven and having returned there, is without beginning or end. He appeared once—a Priest from heaven—to make a one-time sacrifice and bring sinners to a Holy God. Then He made Himself invisible again. He was taken out of our sight (Acts 1:9). He returned to the Father. He is seated at the right hand of the Father until all His enemies are made a footstool for His feet.

Eighth, God confirmed these interpretations of Genesis 14:18-20 with an oath. One thousand years after Melchizedek appeared to Abraham, God used Israel's first righteous King—David—to confirm what Melchizedek revealed to Abraham. The coming of the Righteous King Jesus was another thousand years away, but God spoke through David to confirm Jesus with an oath. It was promised that the Messiah would be a Priest from the order of Melchizedek. It is the only mention of Melchizedek in the Old Testament after Genesis 14.

The Lord has sworn and will not change His mind, "You are a priest forever according to the order of Melchizedek" (Psalm 110:4)

Ninth, and finally, even as Melchizedek disappeared from the text of Genesis without being replaced, Jesus "because He continues forever, holds His priesthood forever" (Hebrews 7:24). God's oath in Psalm 110:4 confirmed Jesus' eternal priesthood. Jesus offered priestly prayers during His days on earth (Hebrews 5:7), but the Jewish rulers thought they put an end to that when they nailed Him to a cross and watched Him die. But bursting forth from the grave, Jesus proved that His Priesthood did not need to be replaced. Levites were weak, and each one needed to be replaced as they died off, generation after generation. Jesus confirmed His eternal priesthood by the power of an indestructible life!

Conclusion

Jesus is the Great and Final High Priest even though Jesus is not a descendant from Levi—the Jewish tribe of Priests. As the Prophet-King David said, the Christ would be a Priest according to the "Order of Melchizedek" (Psalm 110:1-4). In the New Testament book of Hebrews, Jesus is specifically identified as being the Priest to whom David referred, "having become a high priest forever according to the order of Melchizedek" (Hebrews 6:20). The entire seventh chapter of Hebrews goes on to delineate the parallels between Jesus and Melchizedek and the supremacy of Melchizedek's priesthood over Levi's. So, for the nine reasons given, in accordance with the Scriptures, Jesus is the one and only King of Righteousness—the only Priest that has passed through the heavens (Hebrews 4:14) and made a way for you and I to receive mercy and find grace. He made peace between a Holy God and those sinner's who are willing to eat the bread of His flesh and drink the wine of His blood, trusting in Him alone as the Priest who can save us (Isaiah 43:11) and bring us to God (1 Peter 3:18).

APPENDIX D

25 CONVERSATION STARTERS

1. Do you hope to become a God one day? (Isaiah 43:10, 44:6-8, Psalm 90:2)

2. Do you believe that Jesus is Satan's brother? (John 1:1-3, Colossians 1:16, 2 Corinthians 11:3-4)

3. Do you say that works contribute to salvation? (Galatians 1:8, Titus 3:5-8, Ephesians 2:8-10, Romans 4:5, 4:16 versus 2 Nephi 2:10-11, 9:15, 25:23)

4. What qualifies someone to be a priest of the order of Melchizedek? (Hebrews 3:1-4, 4:14-16, 5:1-11, 6:19-7:28, Psalm 110, Genesis 14:18-20)

5. Do you need Temple endowments to attain the highest heaven? (Galatians 2:16-3:14 versus Book of Abraham)

6. Do you participate in secret combinations? (2 Corinthians 11:12-15, 2 Nephi 26:22 written before 1830 versus Joseph becoming a Mason in 1840)

7. What did Peter, James, John, the other 8 and Paul leave behind for church leadership? (Titus 1:1-9, Acts 14:23, 15:23, 20:17, 1 Timothy 3)

8. Why didn't Christ's apostles build temples? (Matthew 24:1-2, John 2:19, 1 Corinthians 3:16, 6:19, 1 Peter 2:5)

9. What do the "plain and precious" parts of Isaiah 29 that allegedly went missing until their reintroduction in 2 Nephi 27 have to say? Since these parts validate Joseph and his witnesses, wouldn't it have made more sense for God to have preserved these portions and let other plain and precious parts go missing? Isn't it odd (and apparently self-serving) that the only thing that Joseph's publication in 1830 restores to Isaiah is this part that validates Joseph as a prophet? Wouldn't it be a weak or unloving God who couldn't or wouldn't protect His Word from generation to generation? (2 Timothy 3:16)

10. Since D&C 132 was written in 1843 but practiced as early as 1831, when did Emma Smith find out about polygamy and did it contradict any plain and precious parts of the Bible or even the Book of Mormon? (Matthew 19:4-6, Leviticus 18:18, even Jacob 2:26-27)

11. Since Joseph married 10 women whose husbands were still alive and married to them, do you think that God may sometimes approve of polyandry as a form of polygamy? (Matthew 19:10-12)

12. Did Joseph lead people to go after other gods, or even try to become Gods? (Deuteronomy 13:1-3 versus King Follett Discourse and Book of Abraham)

13. Did Joseph make any false prophecies about the future? (Deuteronomy 18:20-22 versus D&C 84:4, the time of Christ's return, all nations getting involved in the Civil War, etc) Does D&C 124:49-53 excuse the predictive element of D&C 84:4? If God's decree were to be thwarted by oppressive men, then wouldn't God know that ahead of time and not make a definitive statement about a precise location and time frame for an event to occur? Doesn't "I am the Alpha and Omega, the

beginning and the end. Amen" (D&C 84:120) lose its force if this God depends on man to accomplish what He says "shall" (84:4) happen?

14. Did Joseph bear the evident fruit of a false prophet in disguise? (Matthew 7:15-21 versus unrepentant adultery, polygamy, polyandry, sorcery stones, Masonry, strife, contention, rivalry, lying to Emma, damaging property, shooting at a mob and killing two men)

15. Did Egyptologists confirm Joseph's translation of the Book of Abraham?

16. Did Joseph believe that he was translating from the Kinderhook Plates?

17. Did Jacob 3:5-8 reflect the racism of 19th Century America?

18. Did any excavations near Cumorah turn up evidence of a million-man battle?

19. Was Joseph a treasure hunter charged with glass-looking in 1826?

20. Is the current LDS First Vision story very different from Joseph's first written account?

21. Did Joseph's mom say anything about how she delighted in the stories that Joseph would make up about Native Americans, long before his alleged retrieval of the Book of Mormon?

22. How many points of comparison are there between Ethan Smith's 1823 book entitled "View of the Hebrews" and Joseph Smith's "Book of Mormon", published in 1830?

23. Do Native Americans have similar DNA to Siberians or Israelites?

24. Did the 11 witnesses reliably examine the plates? Did the 3 witnesses and 8 witnesses see the plates with spiritual eyes (the eye of faith) or with "natural bodily eyes" as the question was

later put to them? Did the 8 heft the plates when they were covered or uncovered? Did Martin Harris claim to have walked for three miles with the Lord Jesus who appeared as a deer? What other superstitions did Martin Harris, David Whitmer, Oliver Cowdery and the others talk about? Have you read Stephen Burnett's reason for leaving the church in 1838? "But when I came to hear Martin Harris state in public that he never saw the plates with his natural eyes, only in vision or imagination, neither Oliver nor David, and also that the 8 witnesses never saw them and hesitated to sign that instrument for that reason, but were persuaded to do it, the last pedestal gave way. In my view our foundations were sapped and the entire structure fell a heap of ruins" (Dan Vogel, Early Mormon Documents, Volume 2, 290-293).

25. Do you believe that Joseph Smith must approve of you being admitted into the celestial kingdom? (1 Timothy 2:5 versus Brigham Young, Journal of Discourses, Vol. 7, p. 282-291)

ABOUT THE AUTHOR

Jeff Kliewer resides in New Jersey with his wife and children. He graduated from Dallas Theological Seminary with a Masters in Cross-Cultural Ministry. Since 2004, he has worked as a missionary to Philadelphia, where he has been involved in several church plants. Jeff's life ambition is to know Christ and to make Him known.

www.ingramcontent.com/pod-product-compliance
Lightning Source LLC
LaVergne TN
LVHW041234080426
835508LV00011B/1201